THE CLEVER TODDLER
ACTIVITIES BOOK

This Book
Belongs To

____

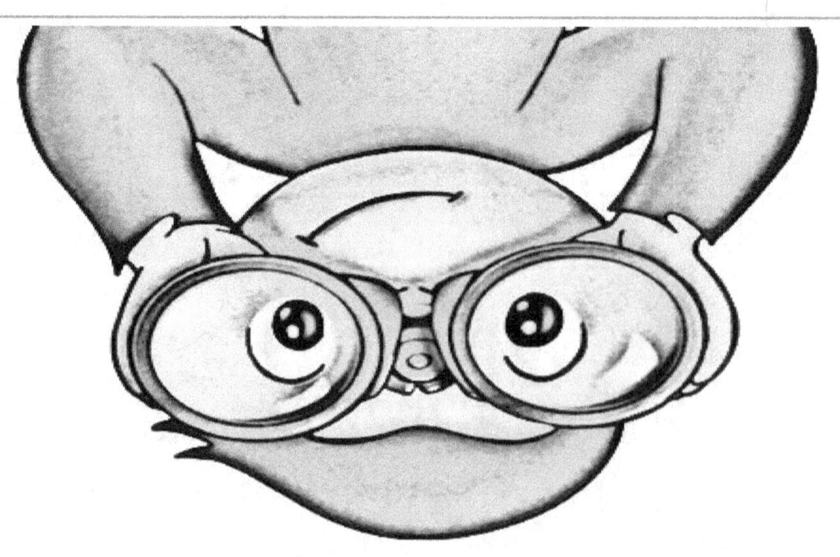

Trace & Color Letters

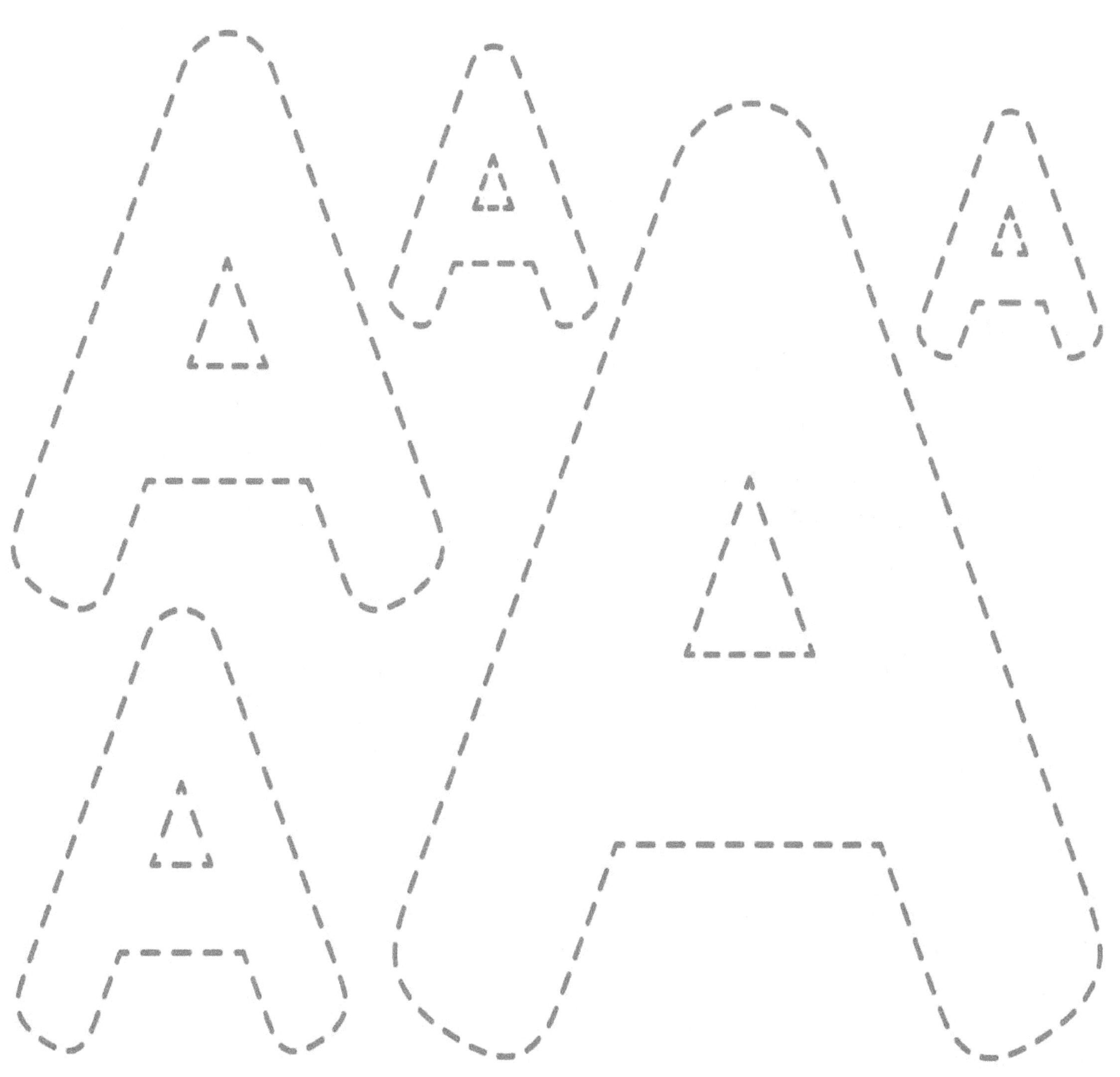

Trace & Color Letters

Trace & Color Letters

Trace & Color Letters

Trace & Color Letters

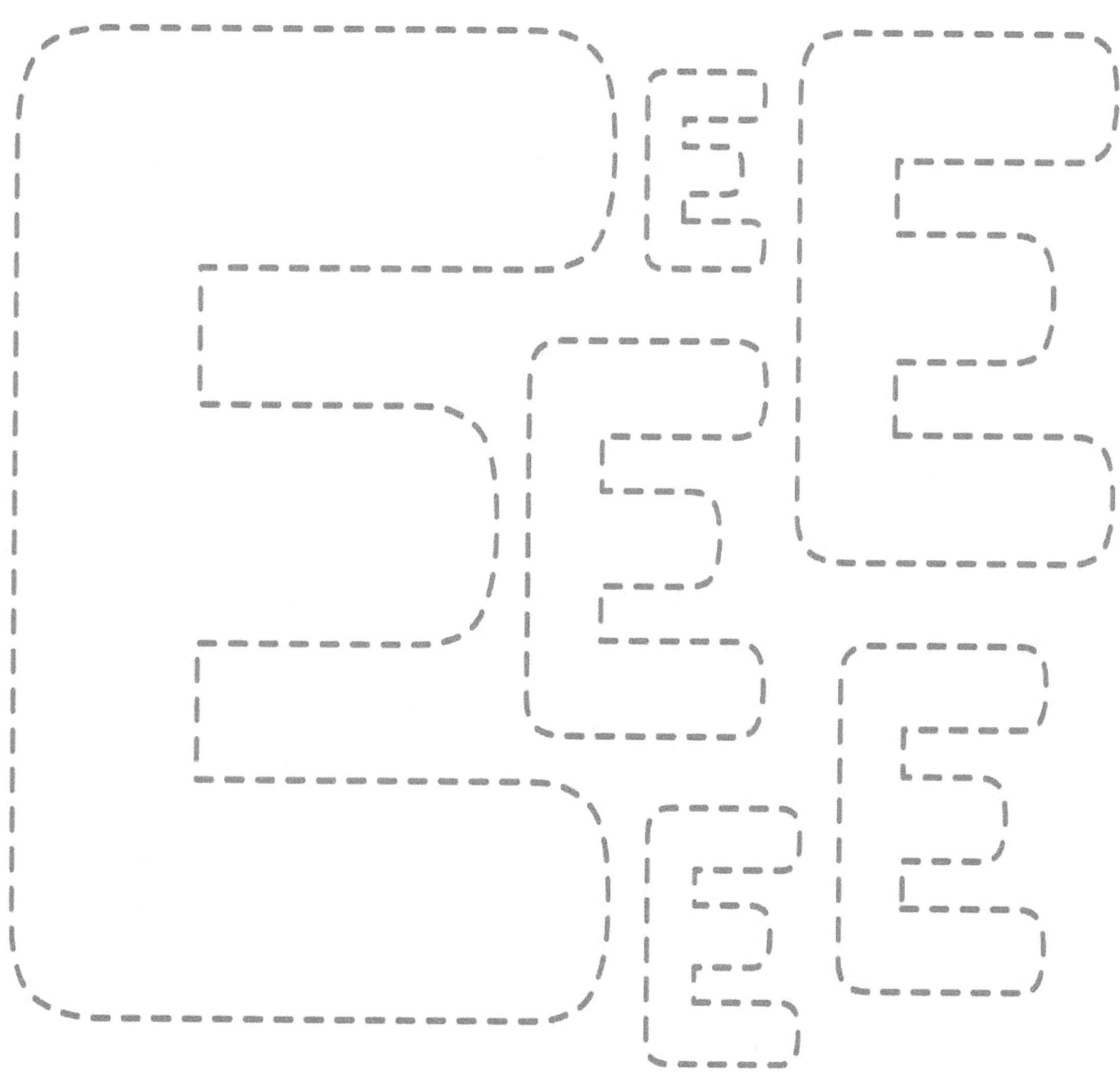

Trace & Color Letters

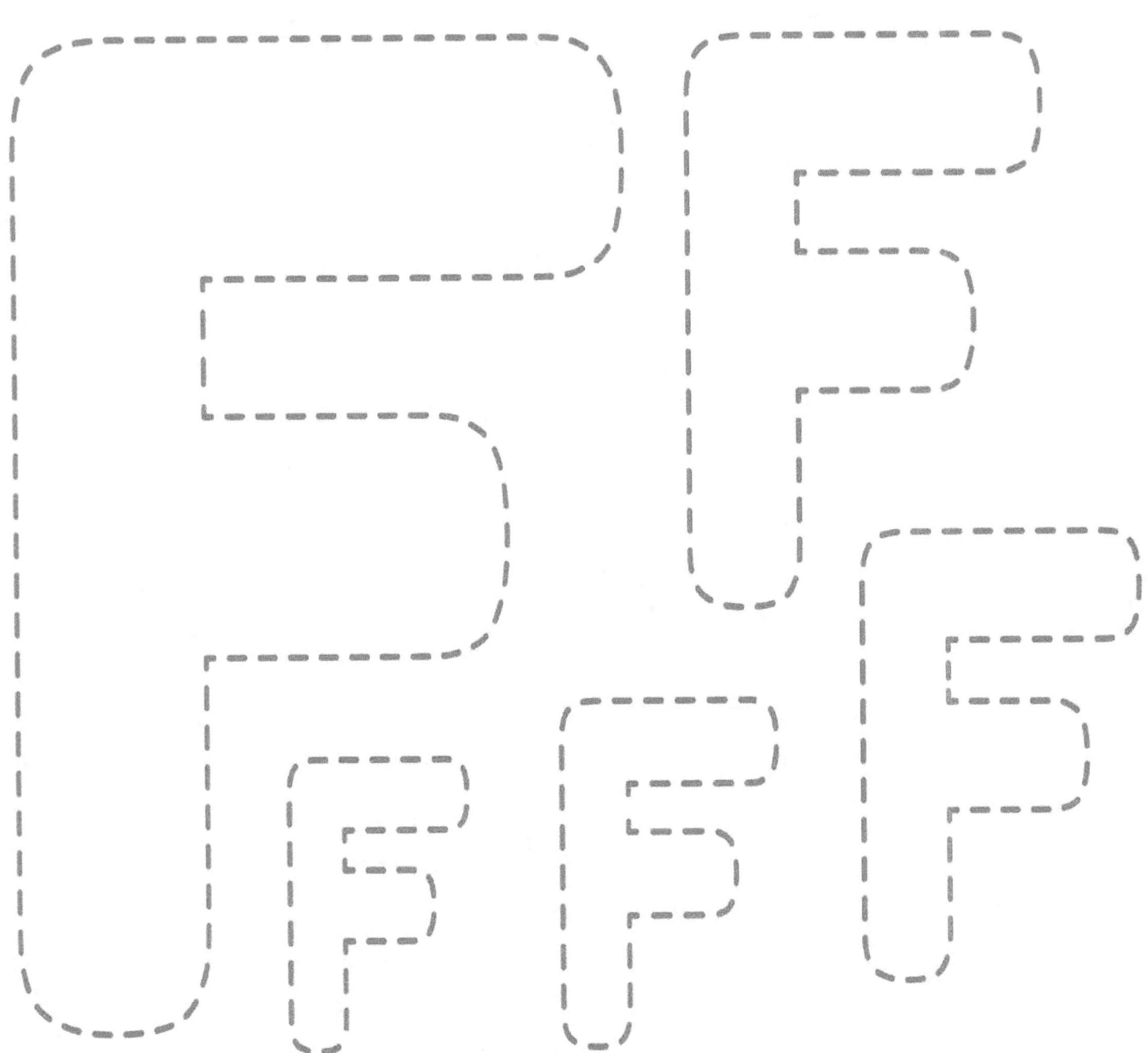

Trace & Color Letters

Trace & Color Letters

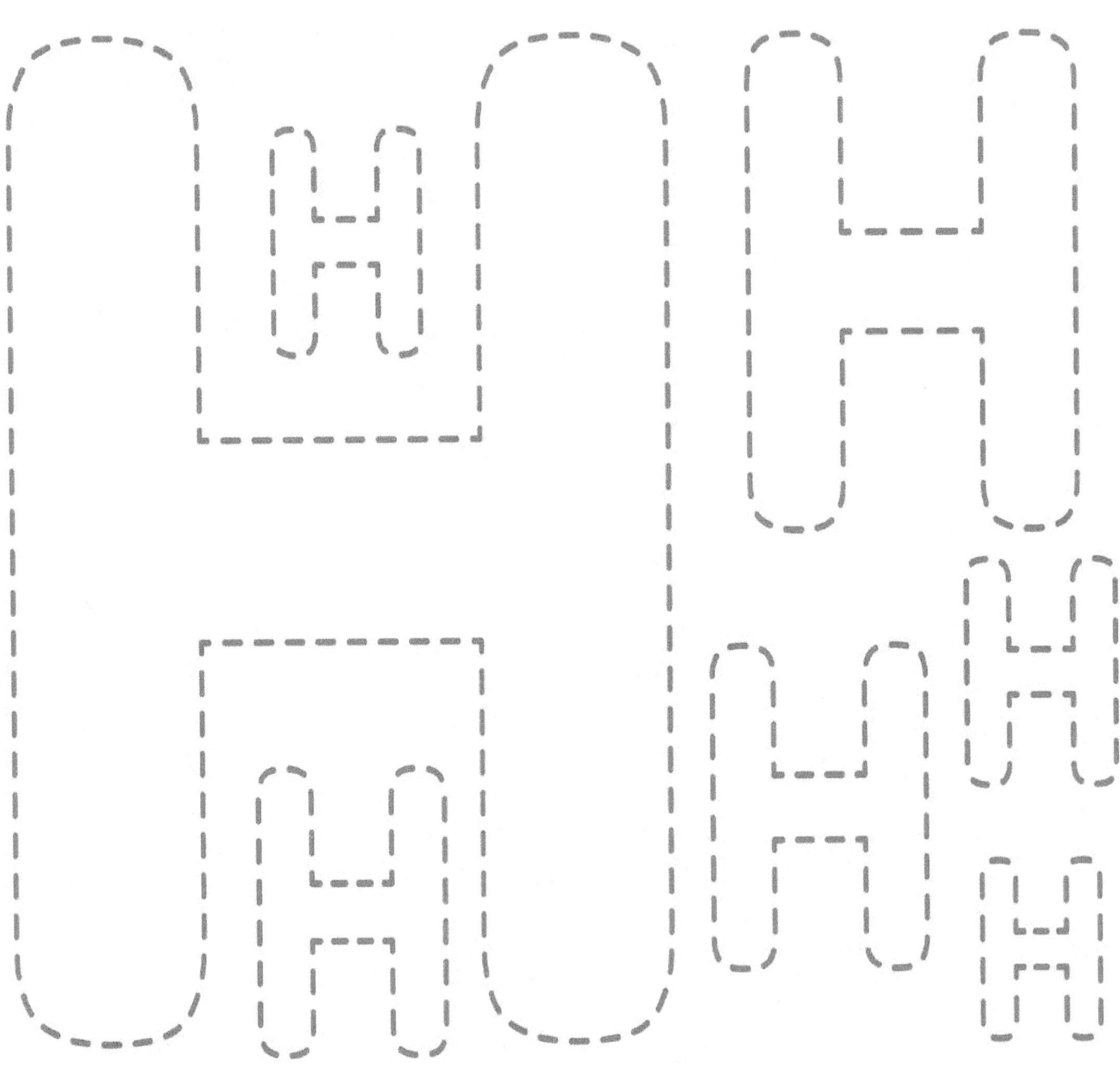

Trace & Color Letters

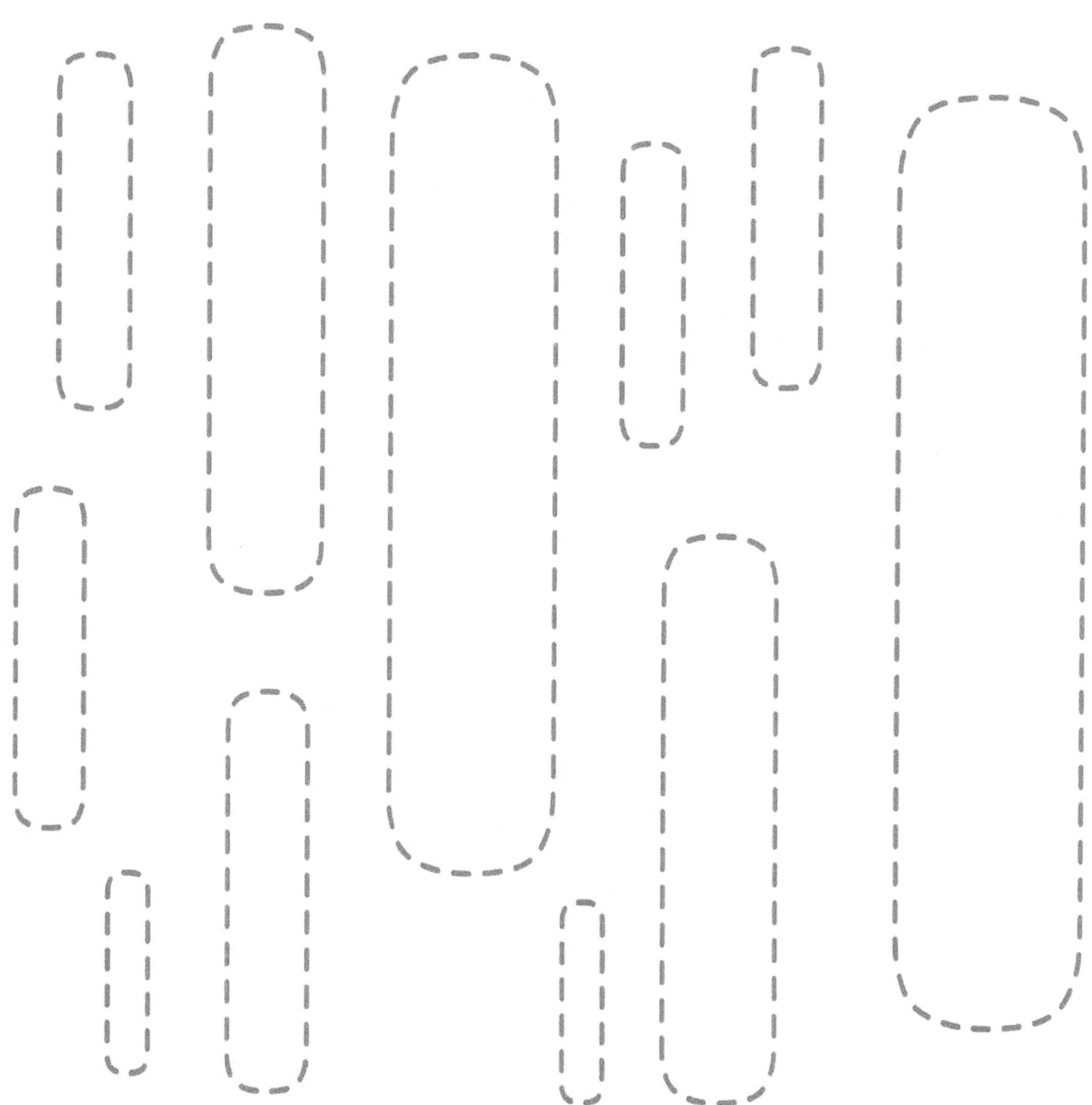

Trace & Color Letters

Trace & Color Letters

Trace & Color Letters

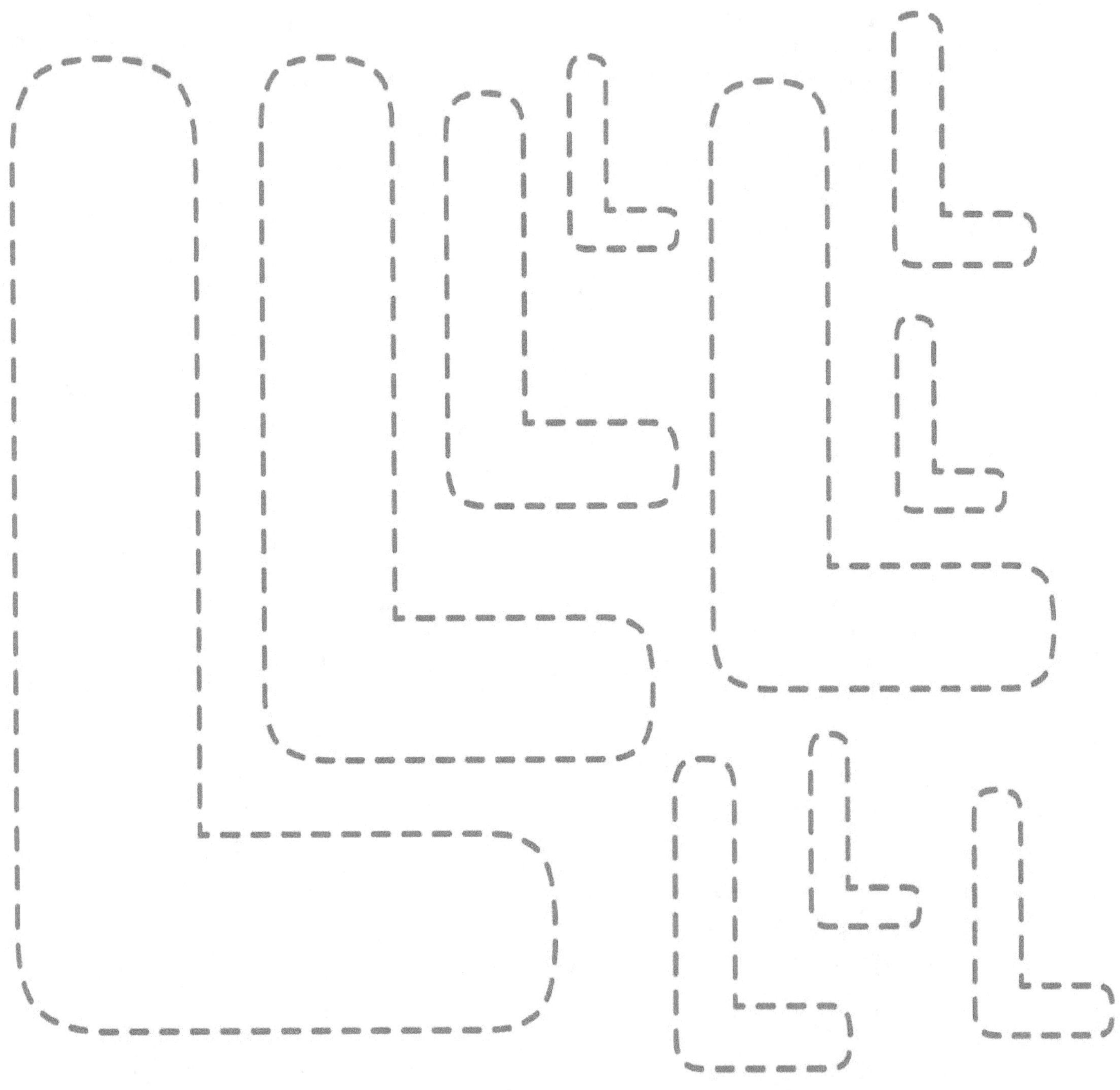

Trace & Color Letters

Trace & Color Letters

Trace & Color Letters

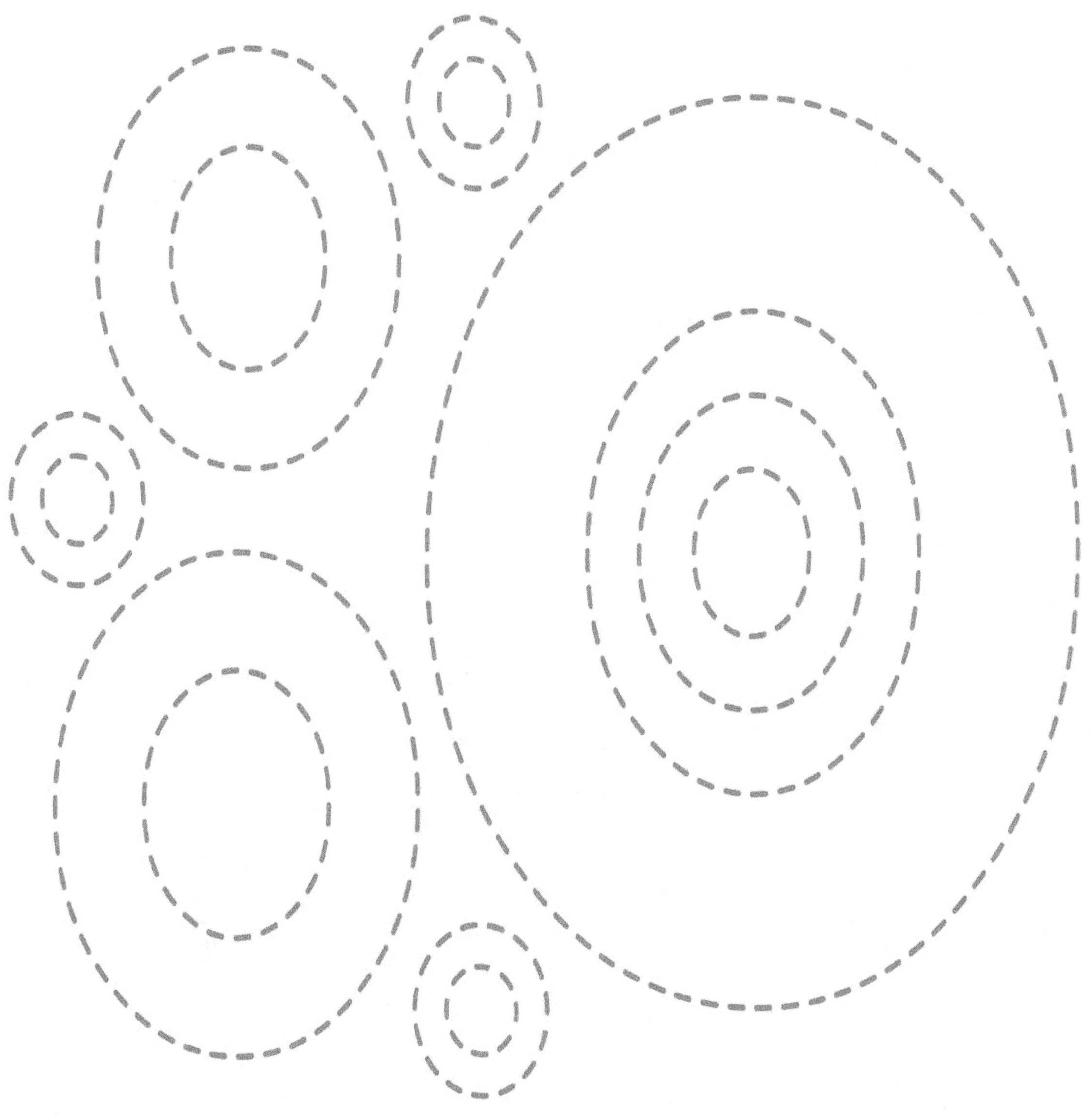

Trace & Color Letters

Trace & Color Letters

Trace & Color Letters

Trace & Color Letters

Trace & Color Letters

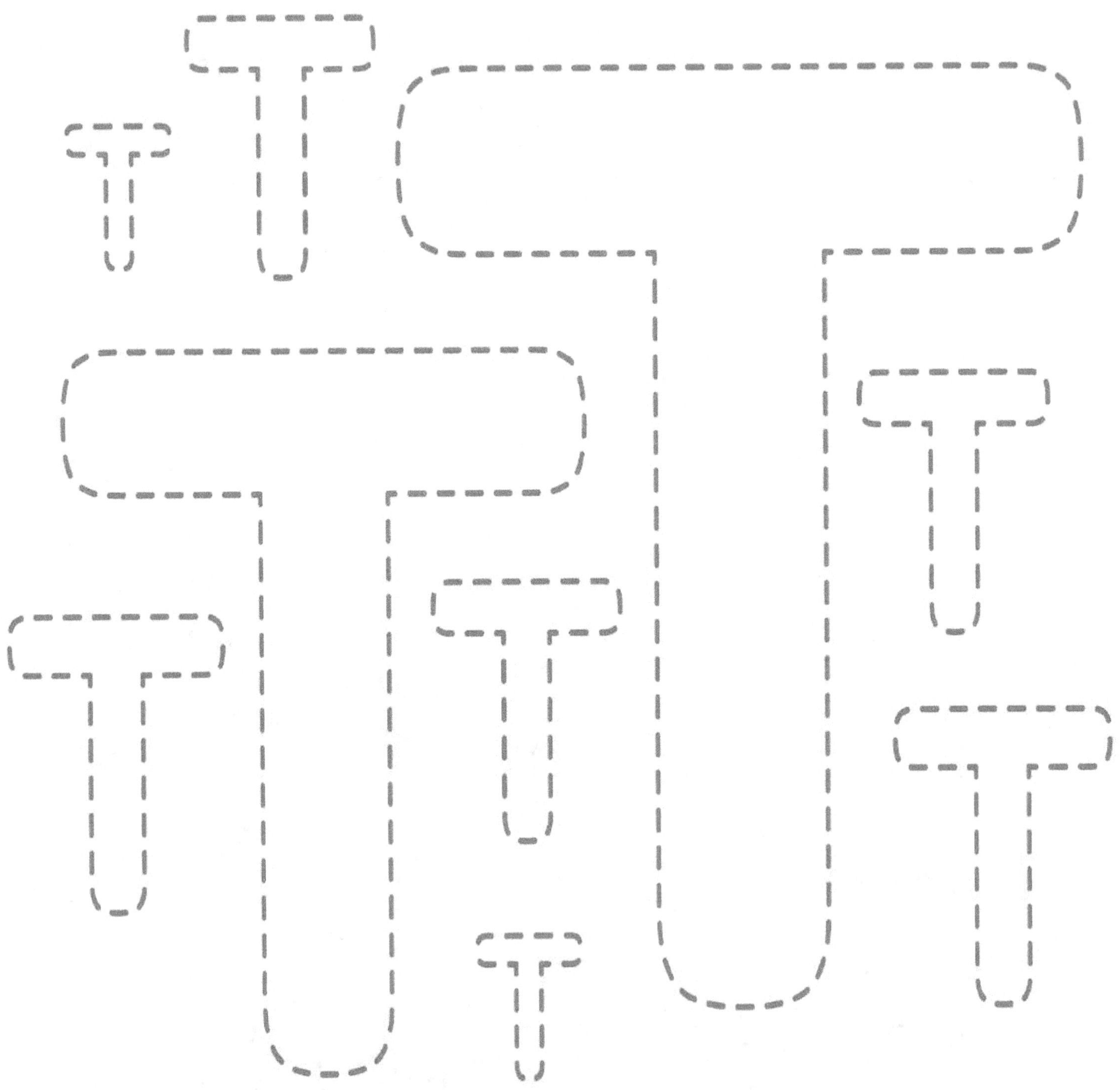

Trace & Color Letters

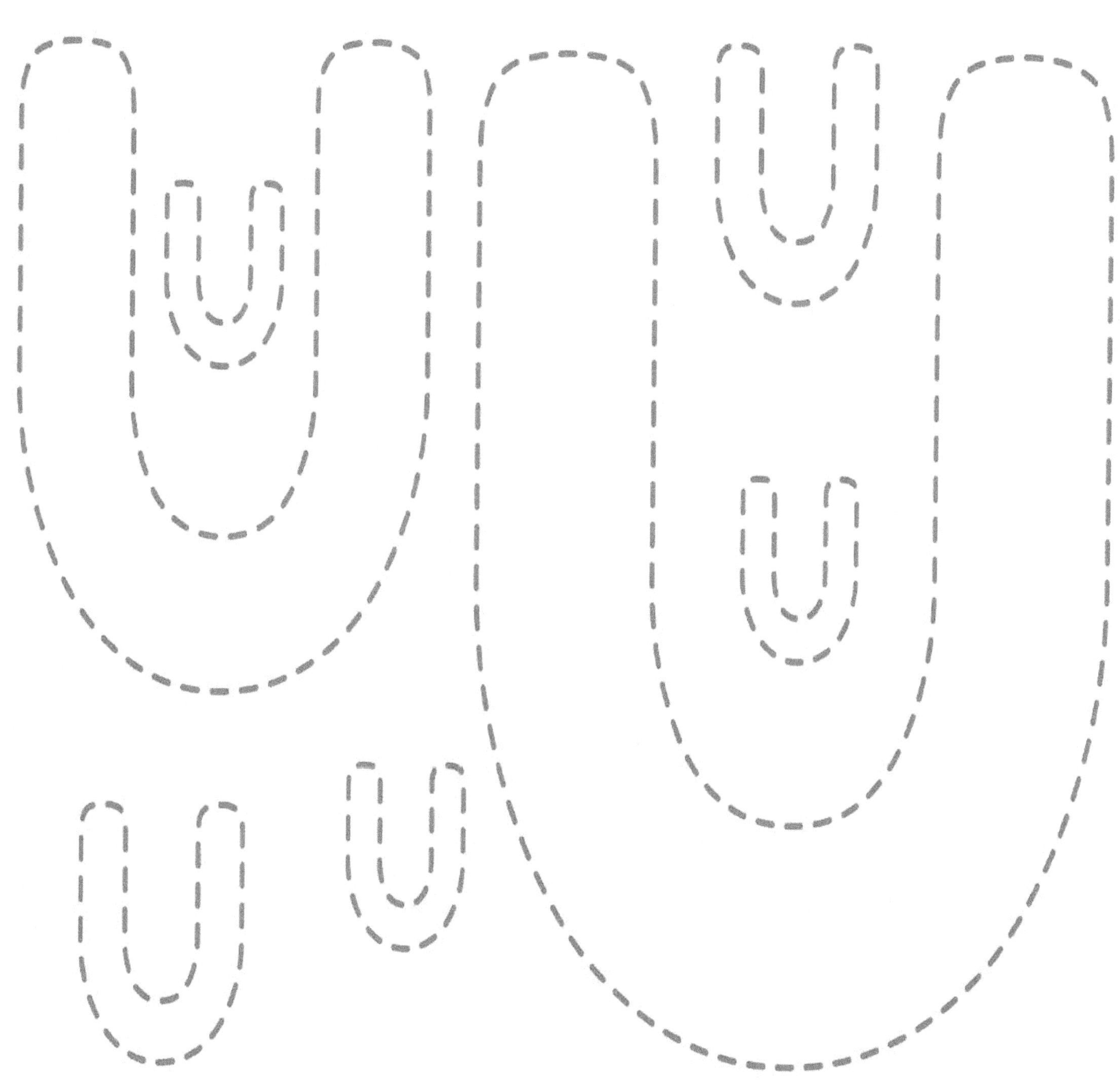

Trace & Color Letters

Trace & Color Letters

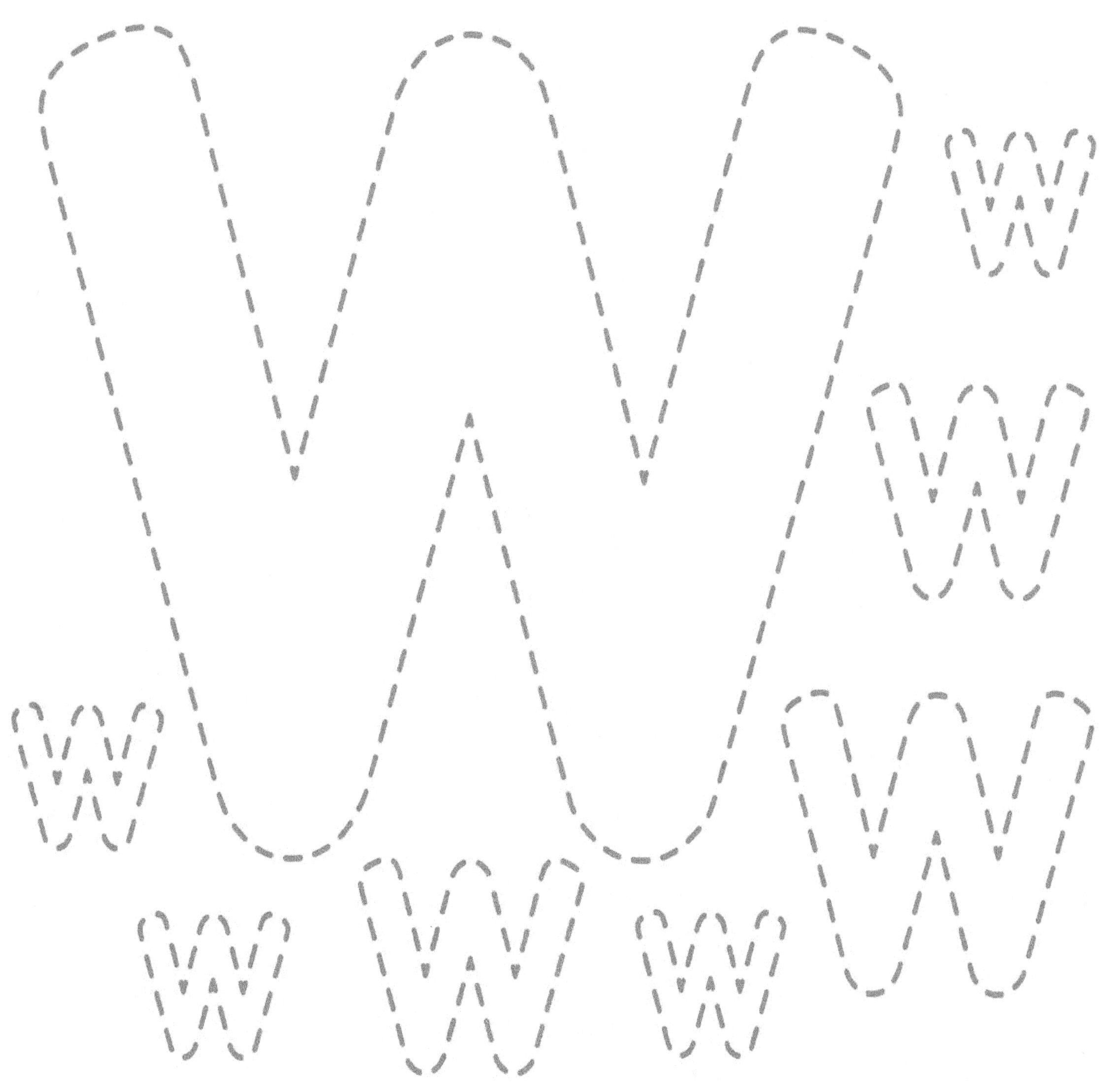

Trace & Color Letters

Trace & Color Letters

Trace & Color Letters

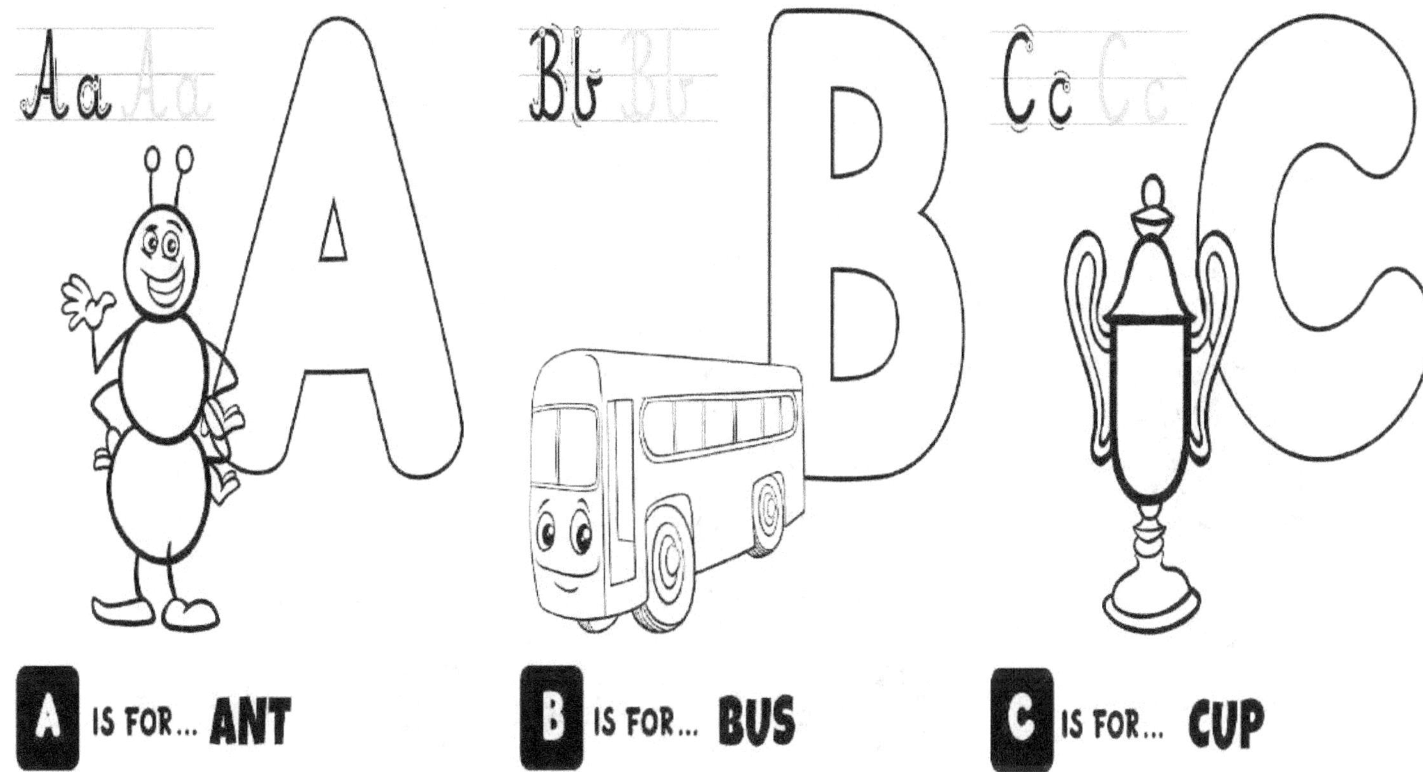

A IS FOR... **ANT**

B IS FOR... **BUS**

C IS FOR... **CUP**

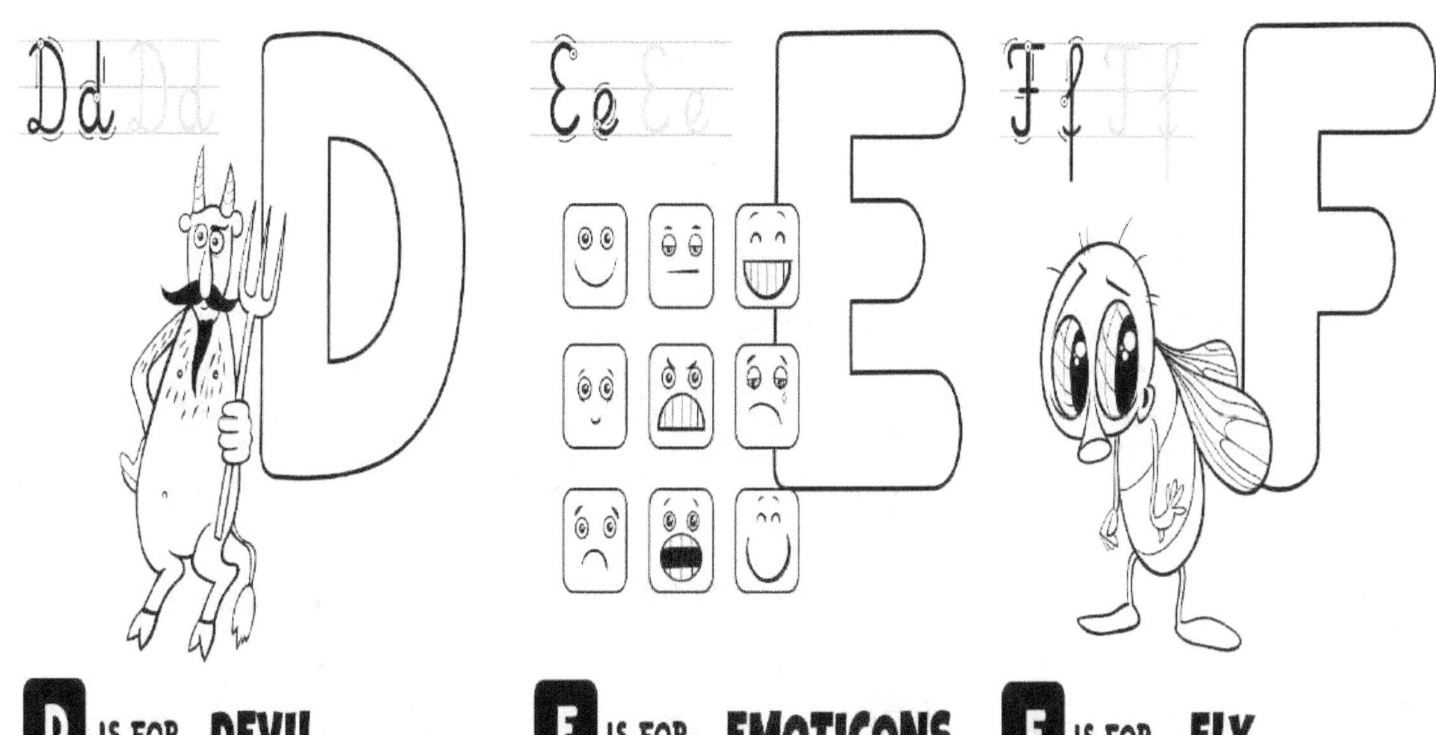

D IS FOR... **DEVIL**

E IS FOR... **EMOTICONS**

F IS FOR... **FLY**

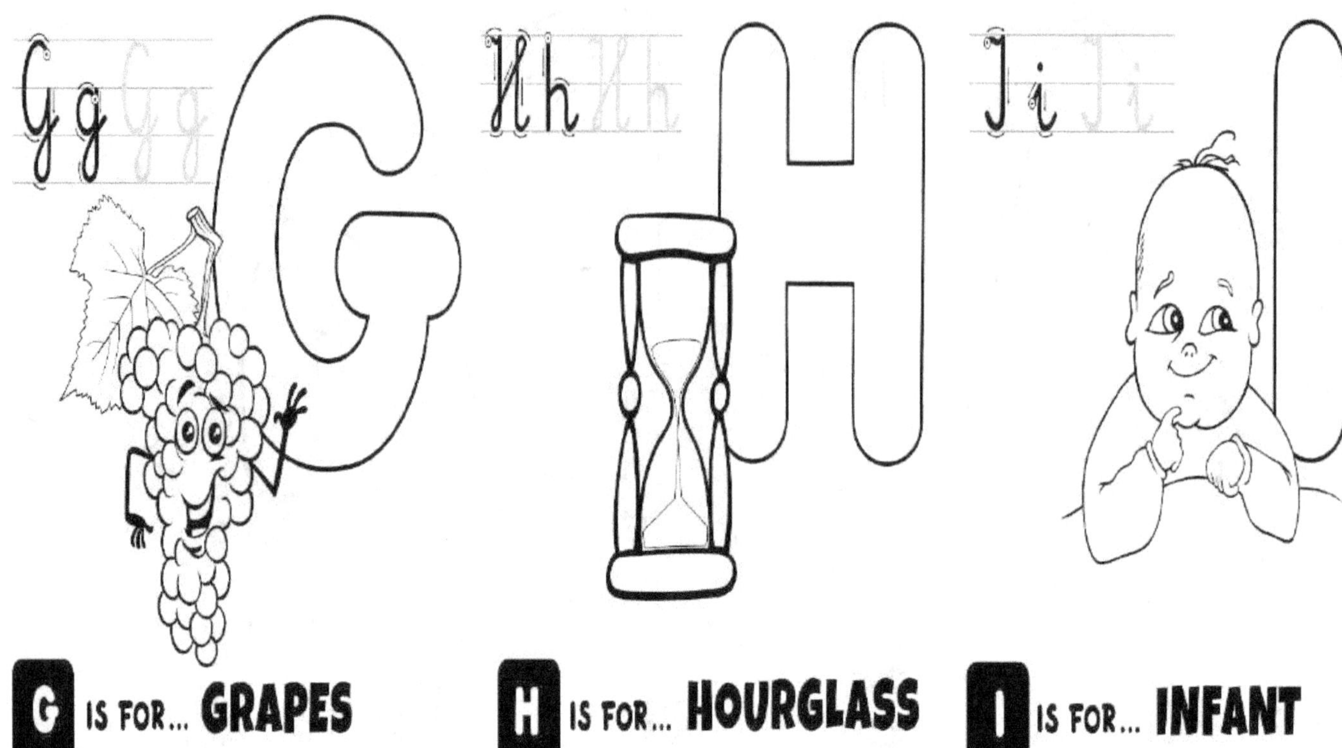

G IS FOR... **GRAPES**

H IS FOR... **HOURGLASS**

I IS FOR... **INFANT**

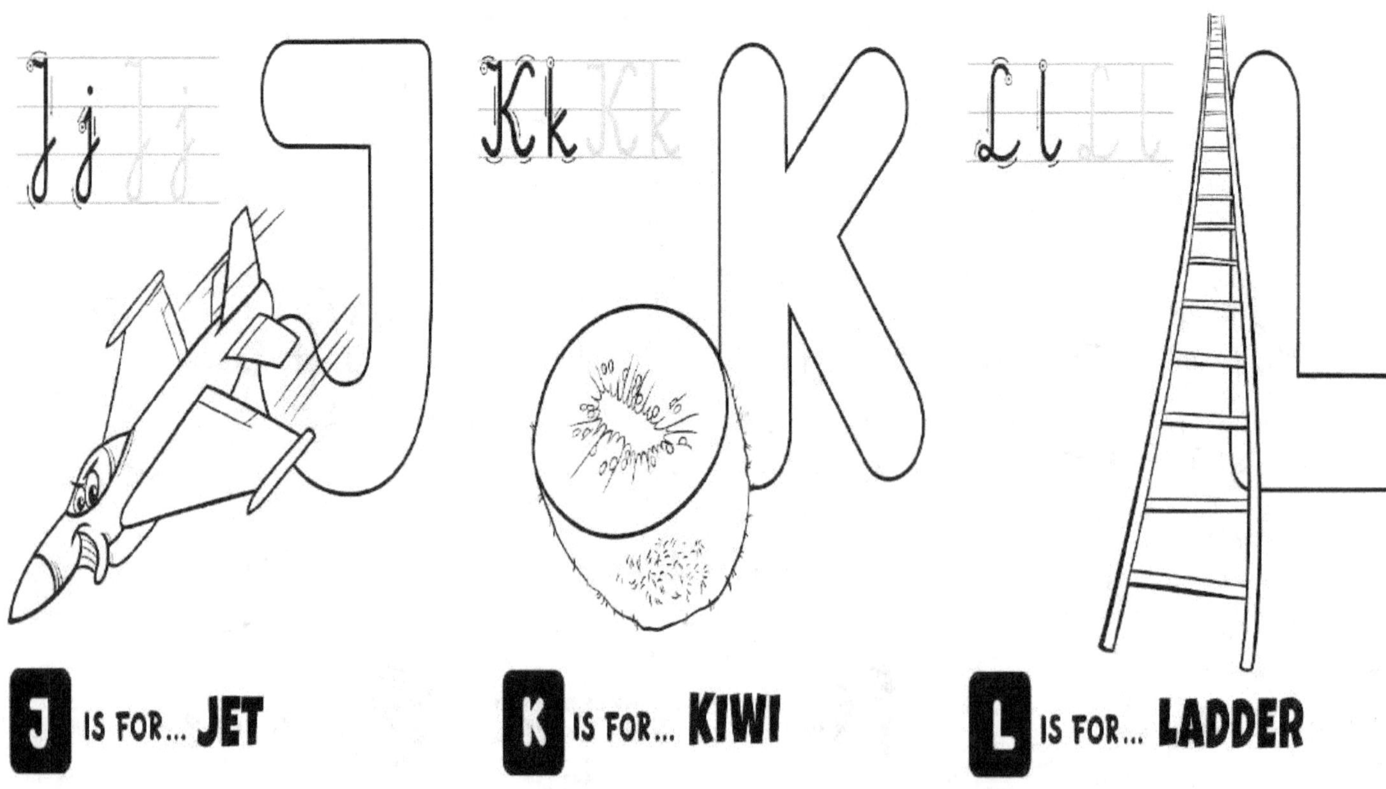

J IS FOR... **JET**

K IS FOR... **KIWI**

L IS FOR... **LADDER**

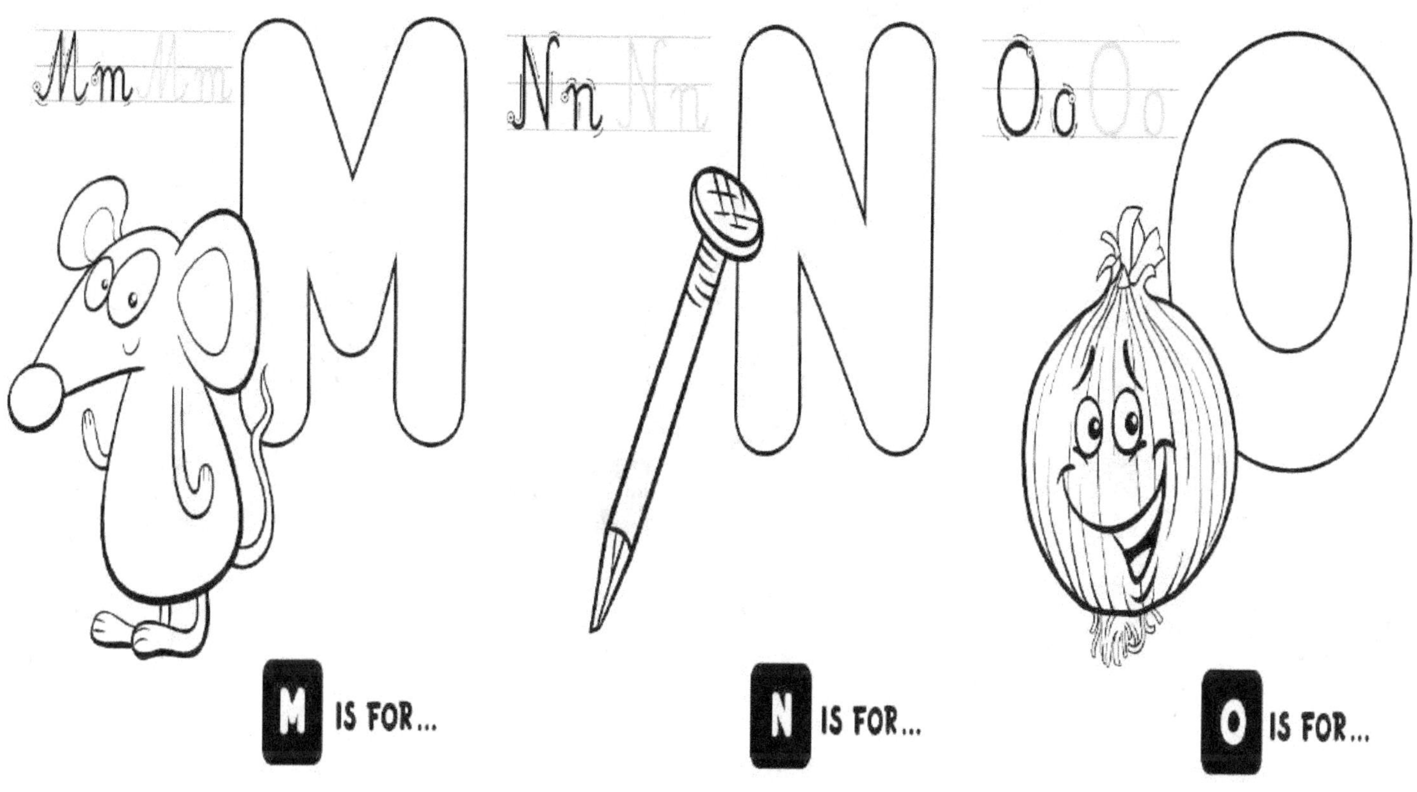

M IS FOR...

N IS FOR...

O IS FOR...

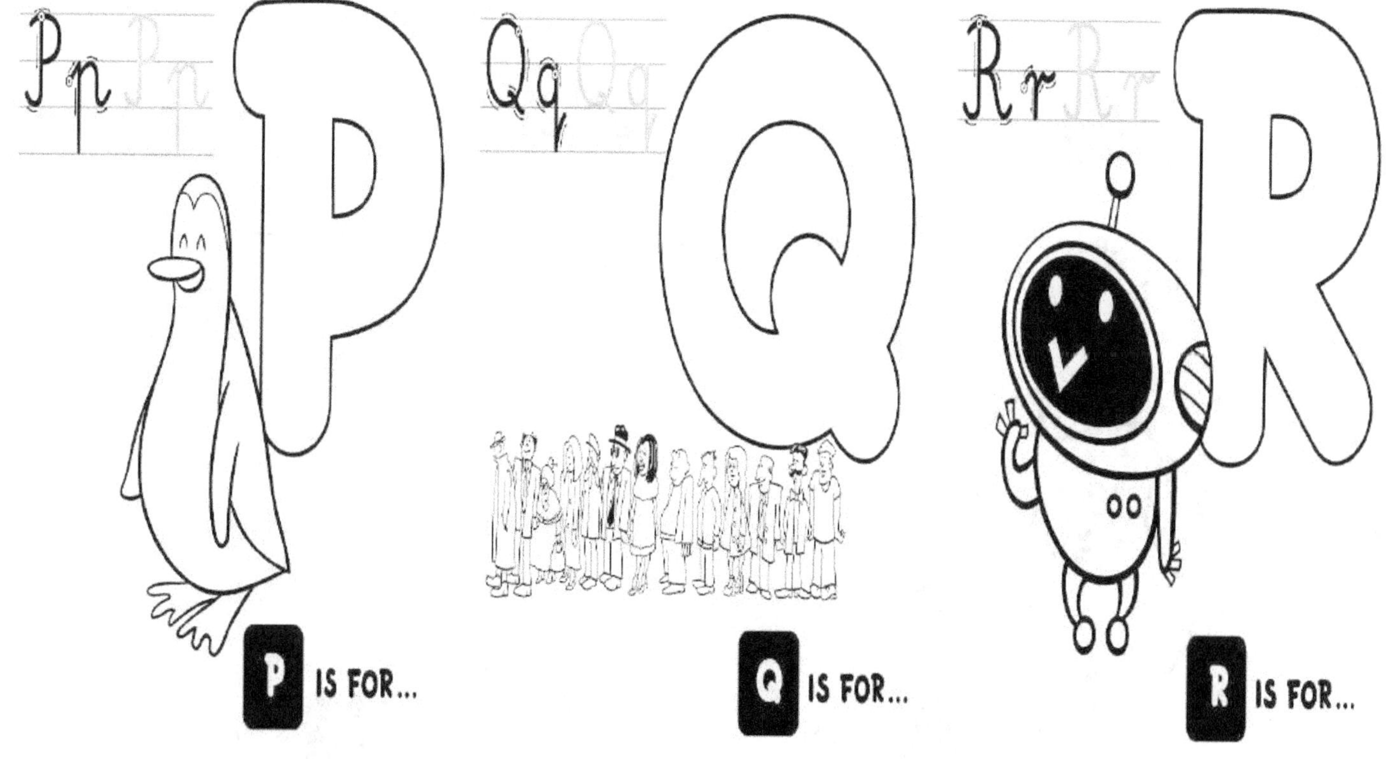

P IS FOR...

Q IS FOR...

R IS FOR...

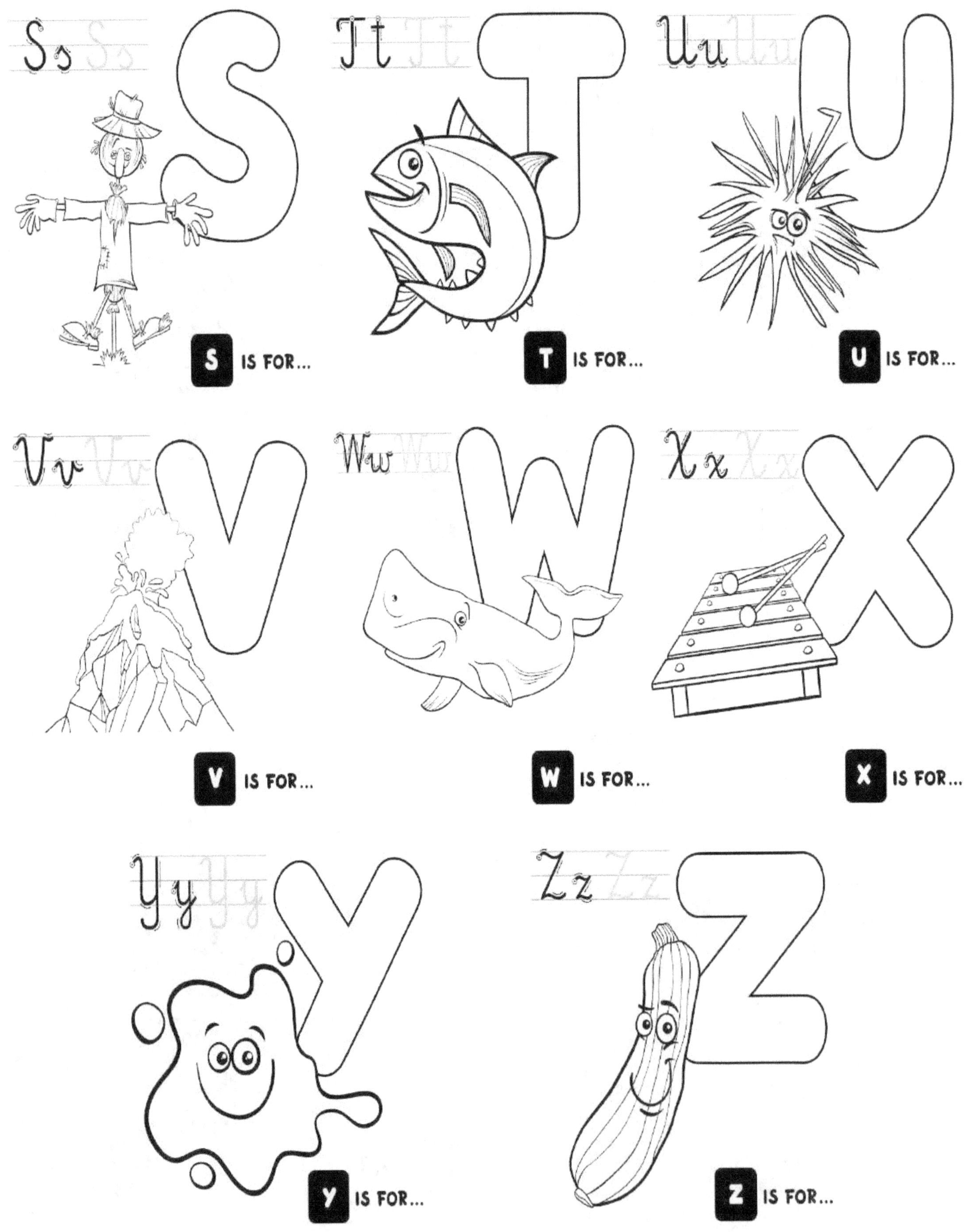

Ss
S IS FOR...
Tt
T IS FOR...
Uu
U IS FOR...
Vv
V IS FOR...
Ww
W IS FOR...
Xx
X IS FOR...
Yy
Y IS FOR...
Zz
Z IS FOR...

Trace & Color Numbers

Trace & Color Numbers

Trace & Color Numbers

Trace & Color Numbers

Trace & Color Numbers

Trace & Color Numbers

Trace & Color Numbers

Trace & Color Numbers

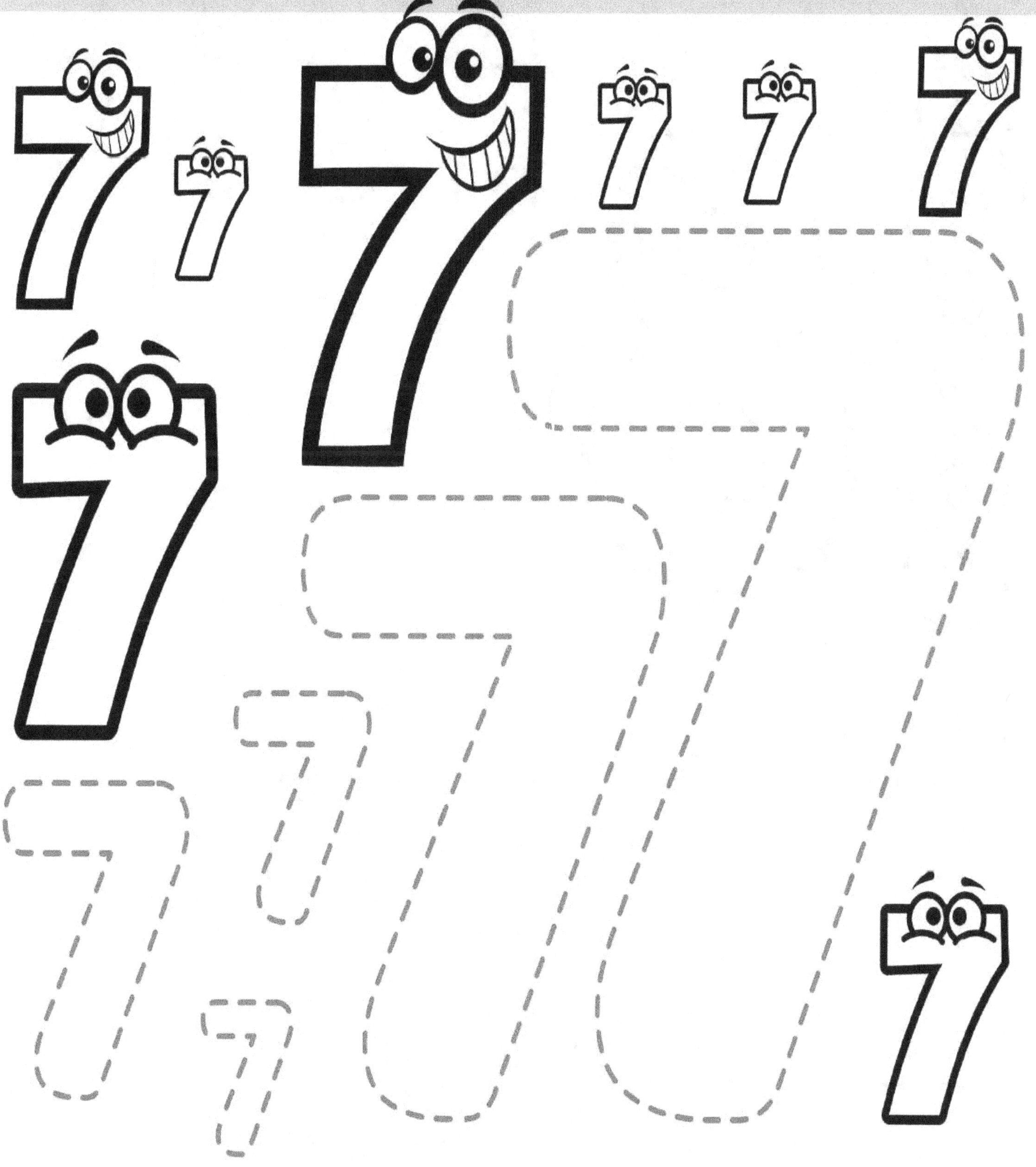

Trace & Color Numbers

Trace & Color Numbers

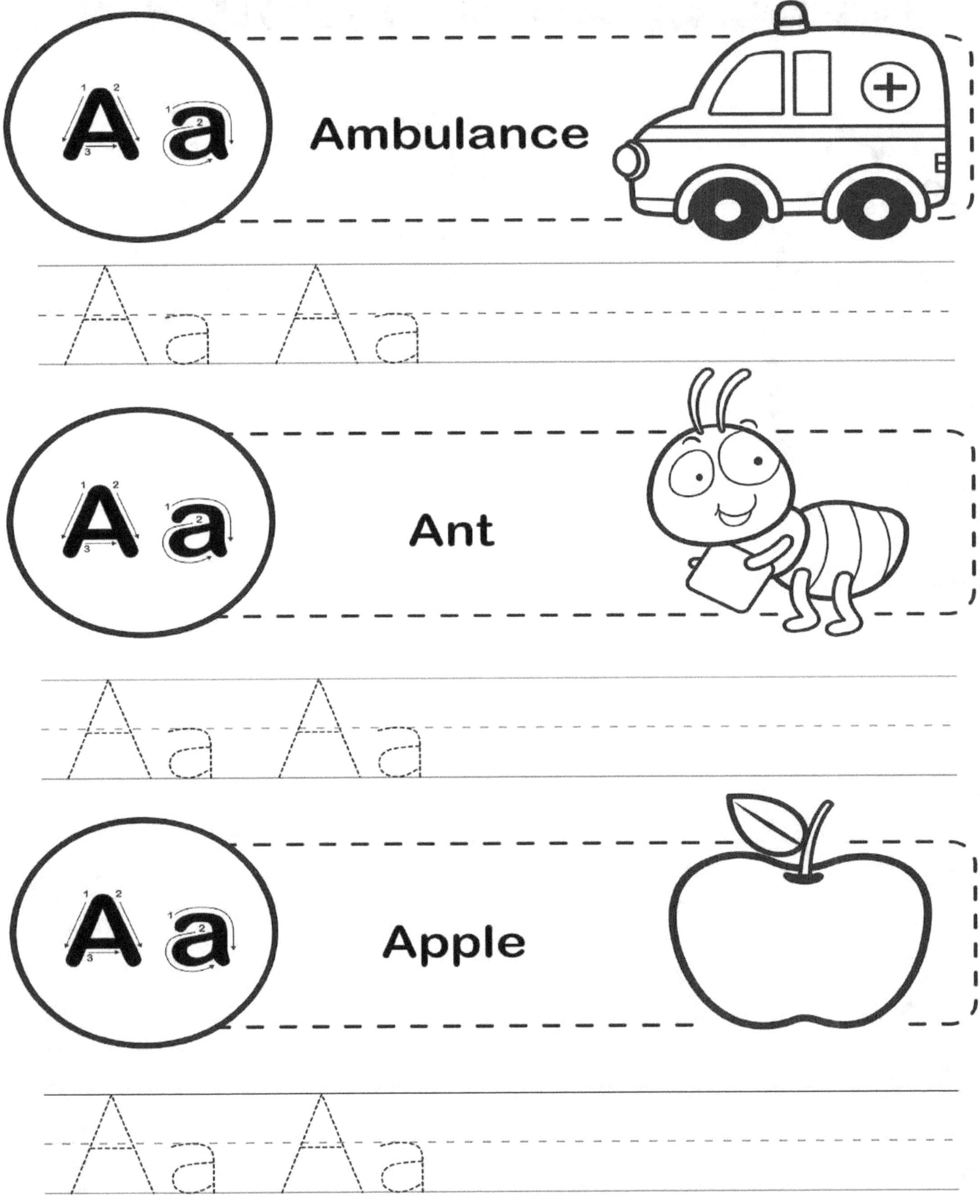
Ambulance
Ant
Apple

Read,Trace,Write and read the words again.Color the picture.
Bb
Bee
Bb
Bag
Bb
Banana

C c
Chicken
C c
Cherry
C c
Cake

Dd
Door
Dd
Dinosaur
Dd
Dragon Fruit

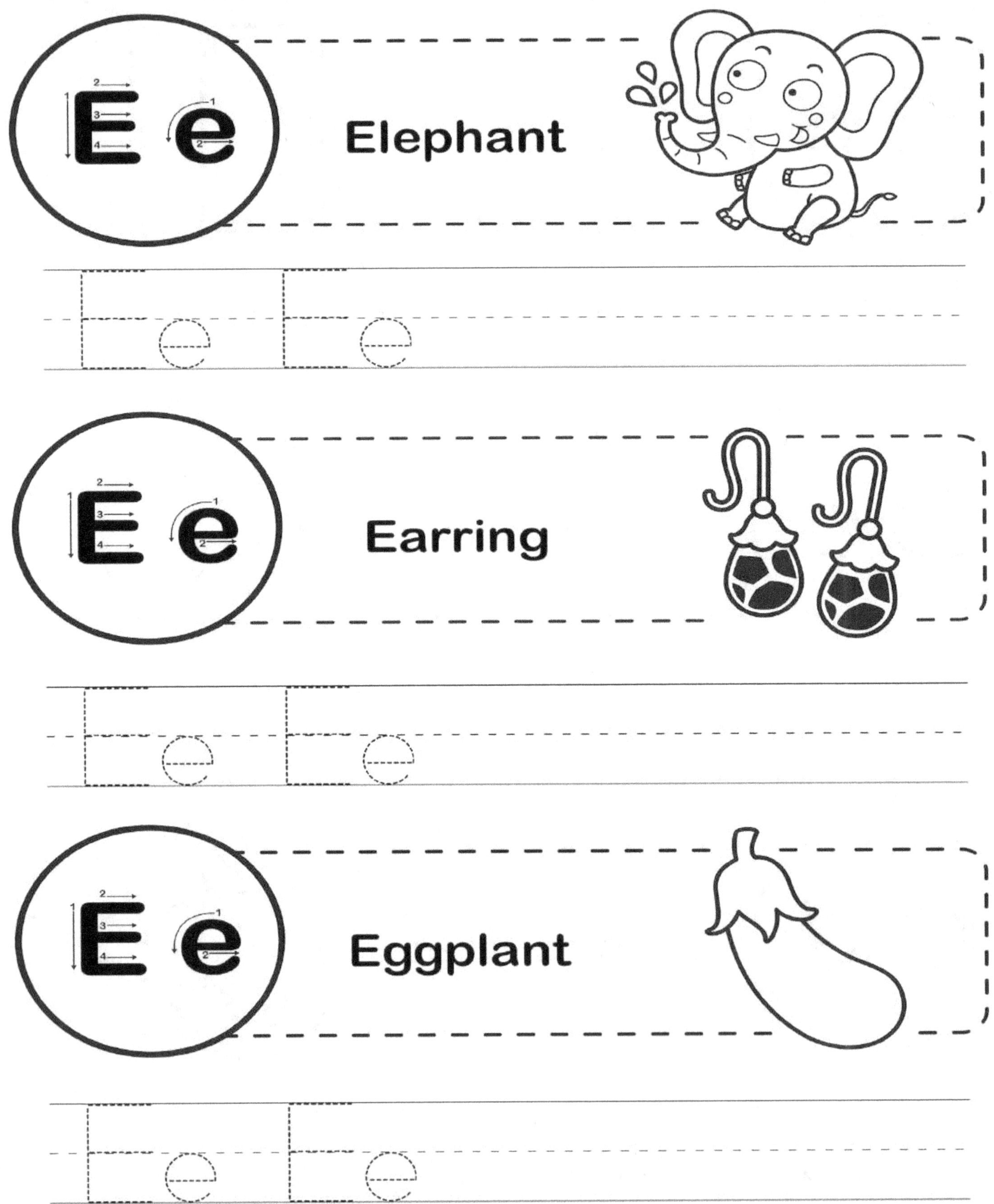

E e
Elephant
E e
Earring
E e
Eggplant

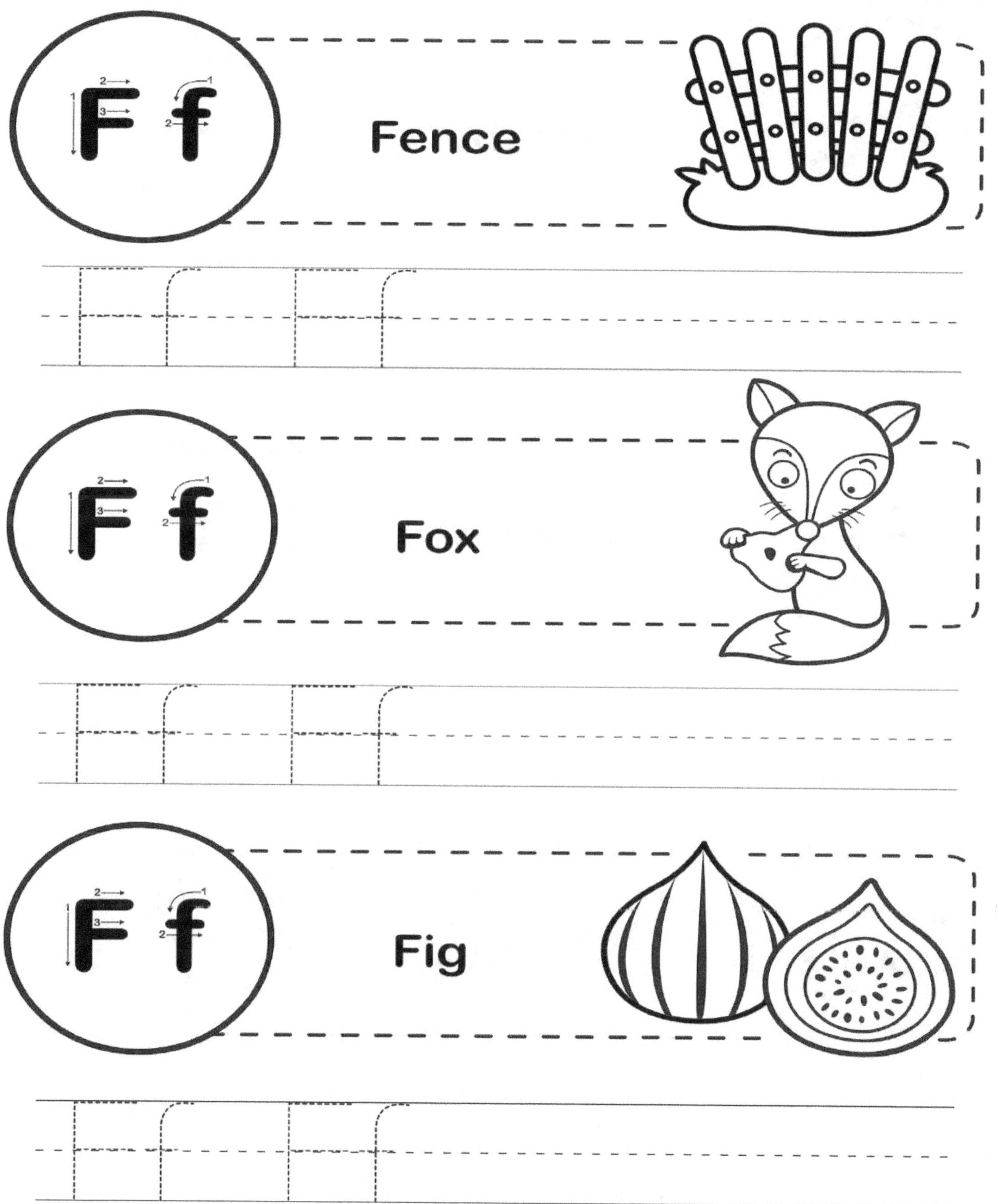

F f
Fence
F f
Fox
F f
Fig

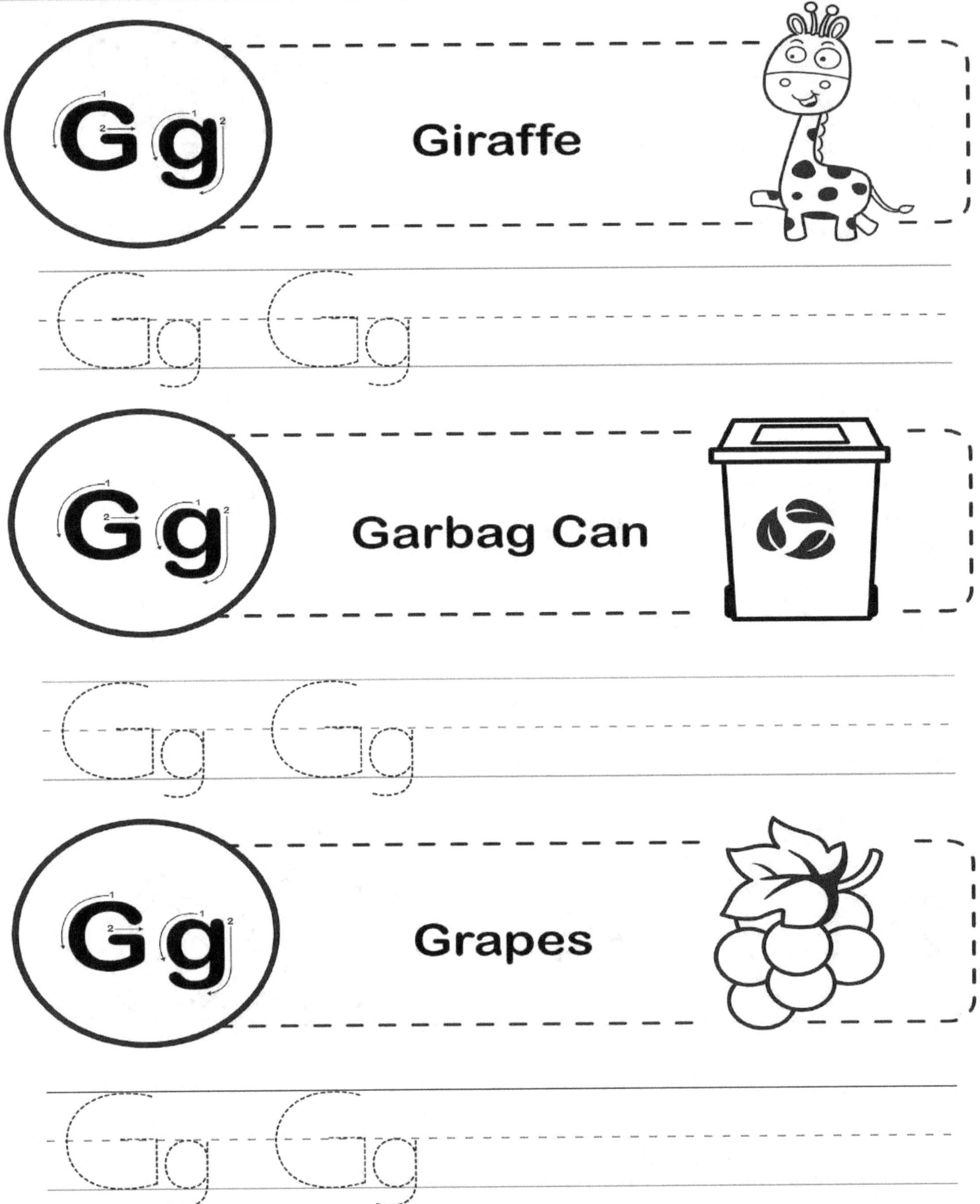

G g
Giraffe
G g
Garbag Can
G g
Grapes

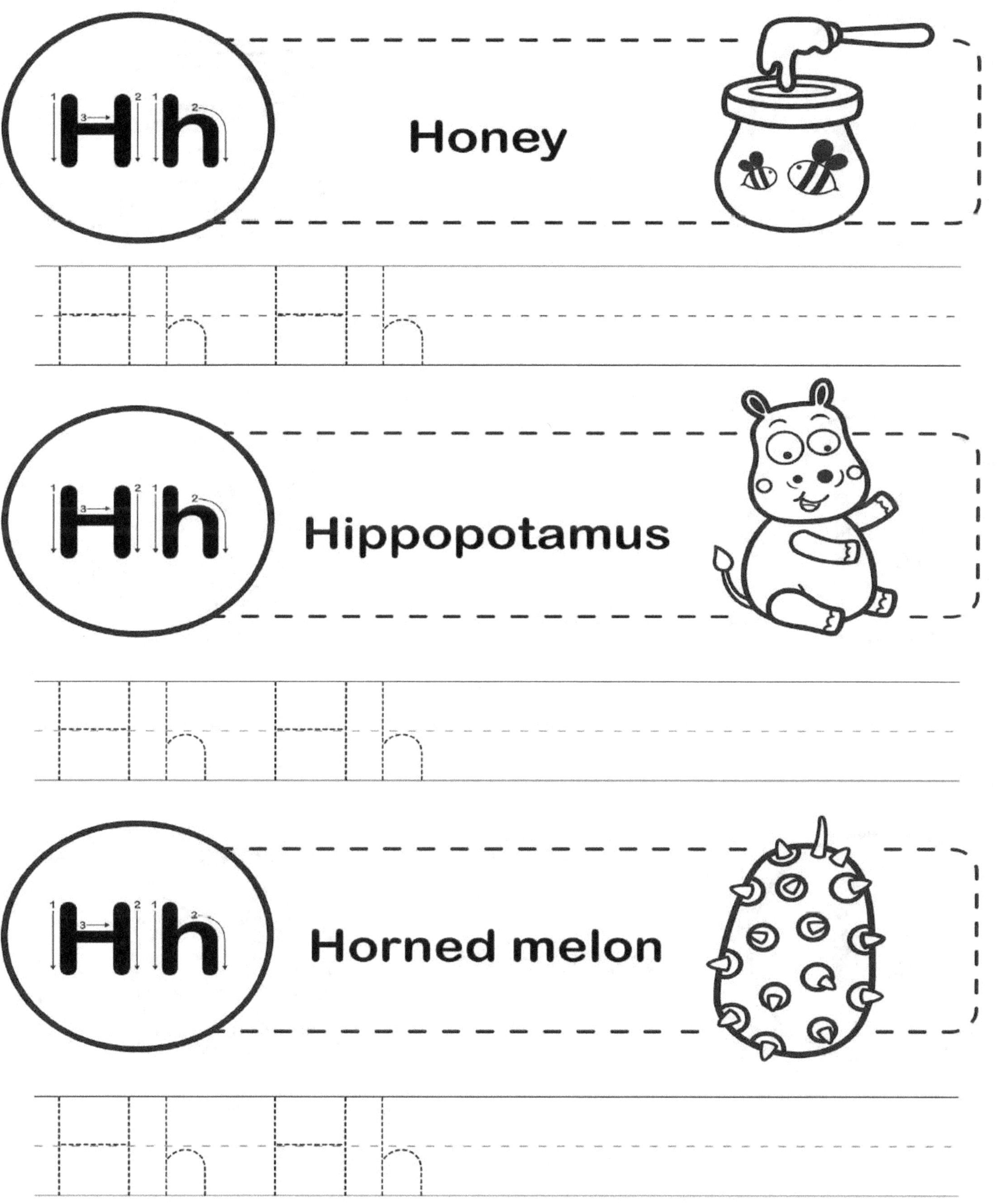
Honey
Hippopotamus
Horned melon

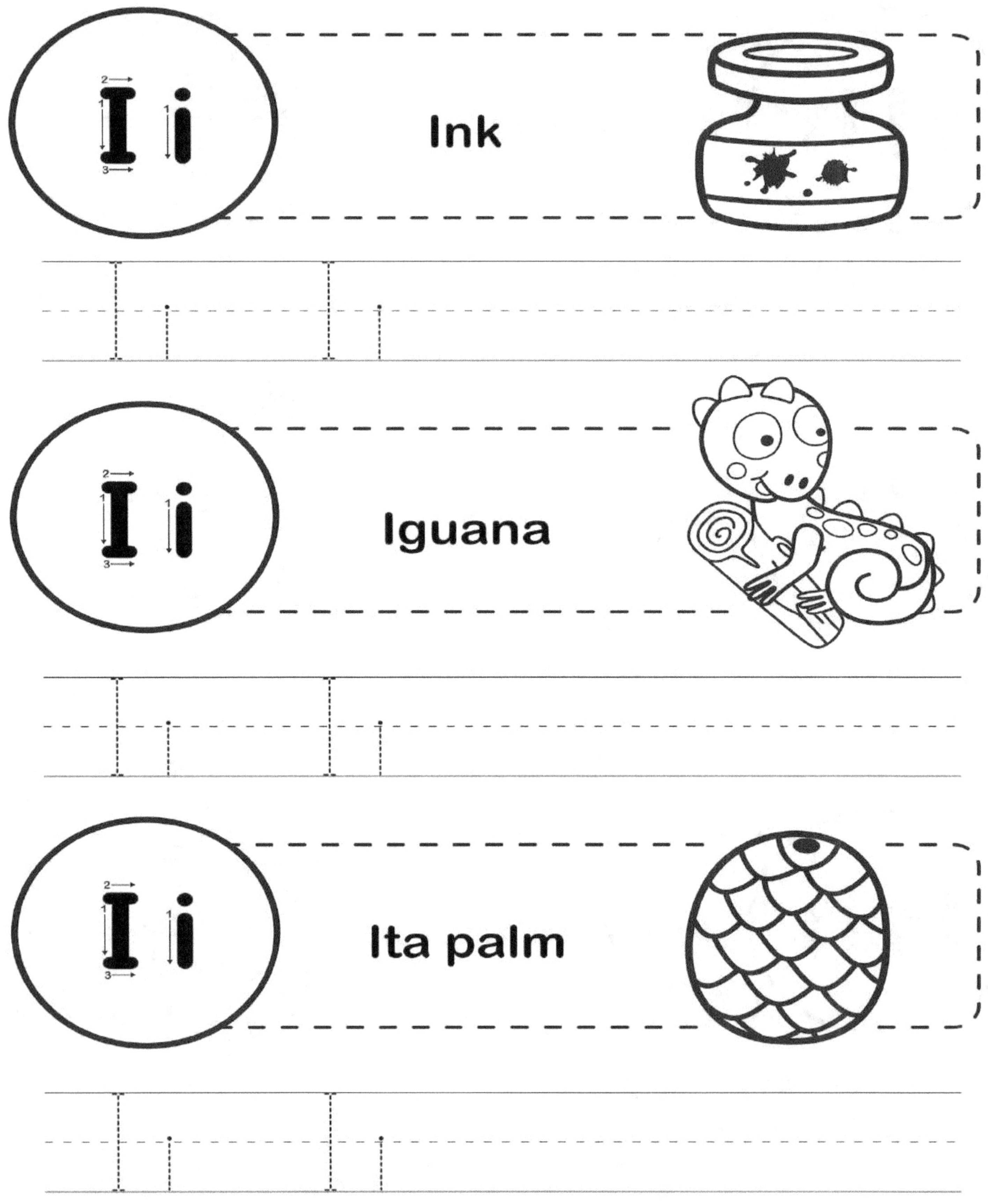
Ink
Iguana
Ita palm

J j   Jelly

J j   Jellyfish

J j   Jackfruit

K k
Kettle
K k
Kangaroo
K k
Kiwi

L l
Log
L l
Lion
L l
Lemon

M m
Mask
M m
Monkey
M m
Mango

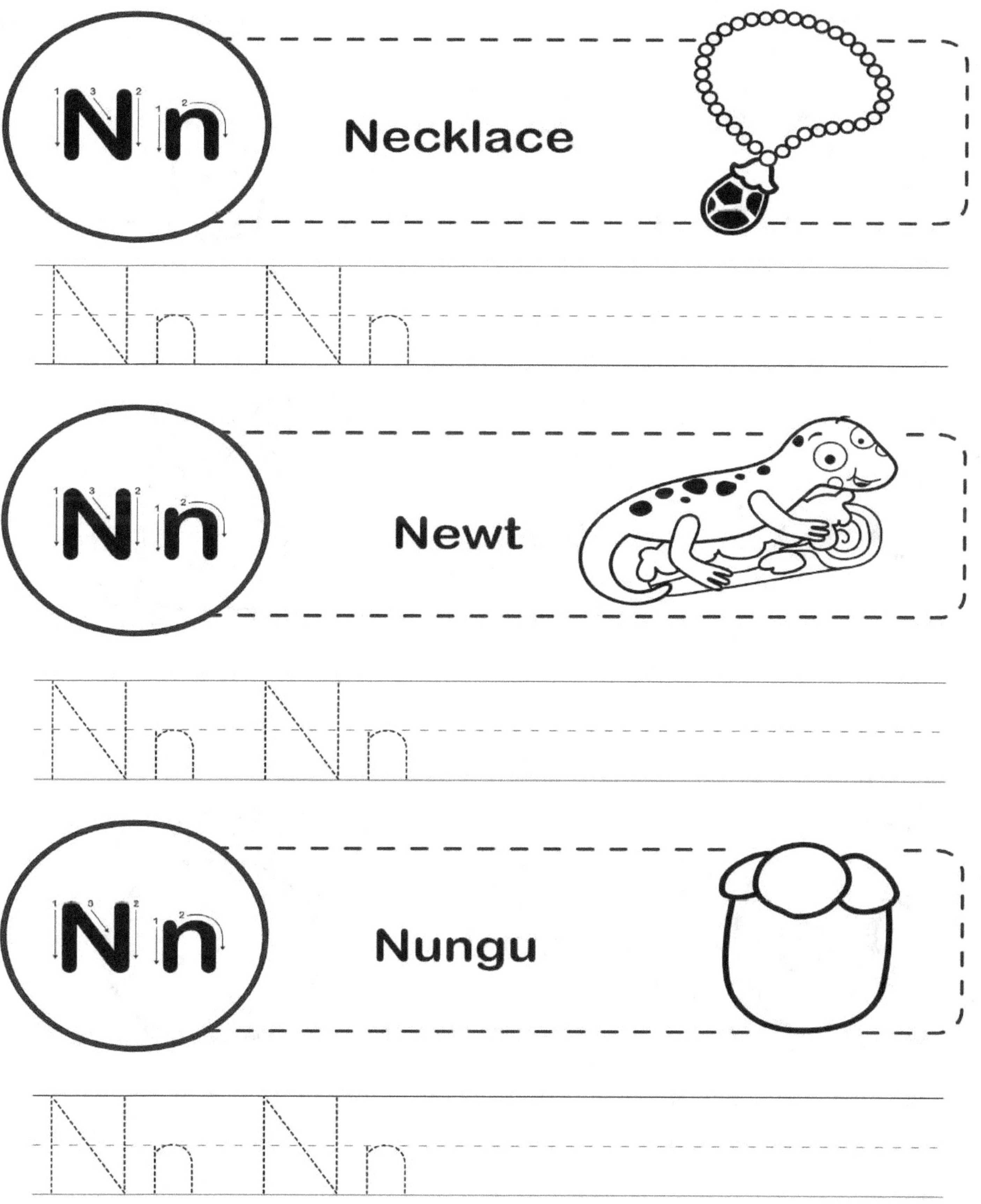

Necklace
Newt
Nungu

Oil

Owl

Orange

Palette

Pig

Pineapple

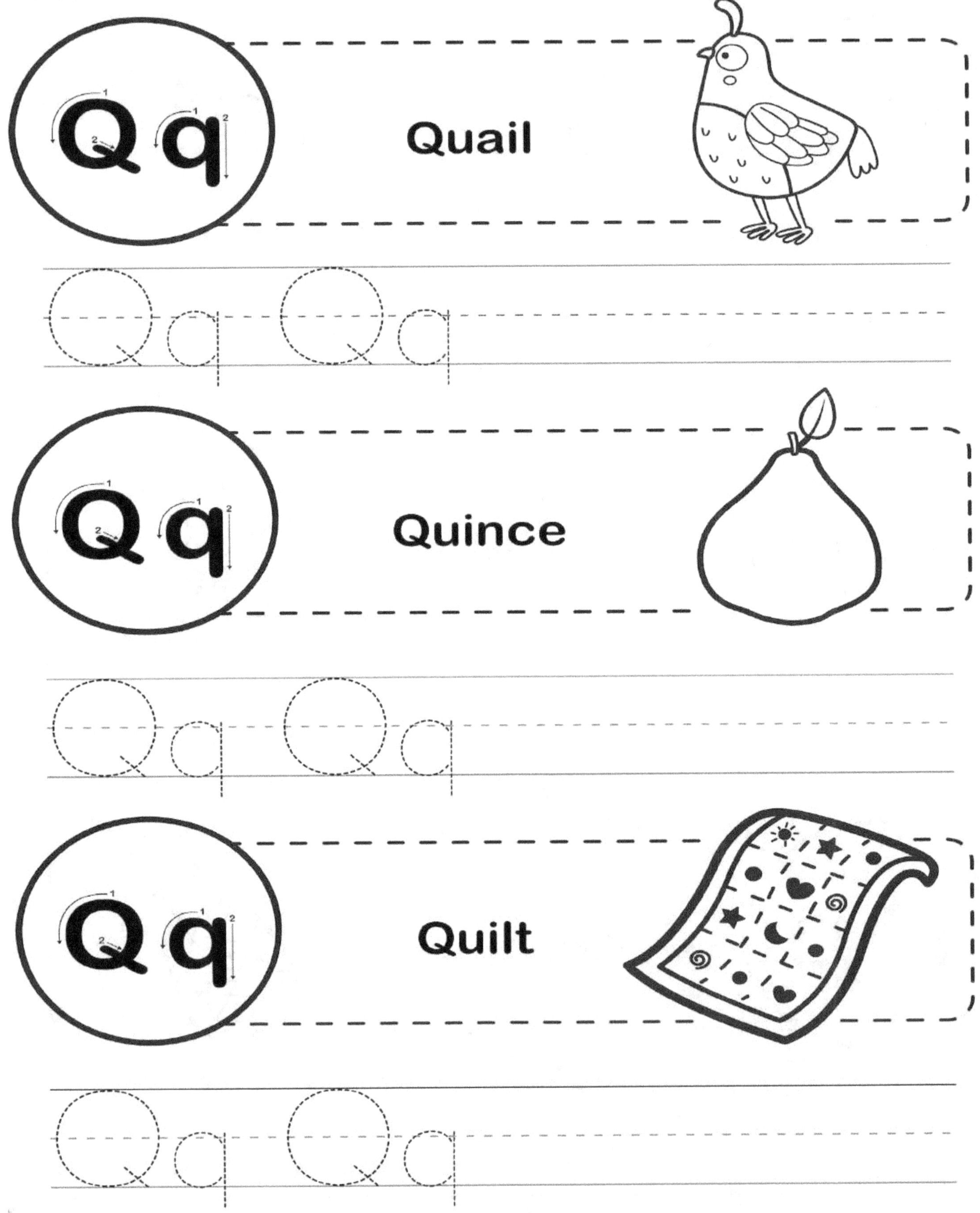

Q q
Quail
Q q
Quince
Q q
Quilt

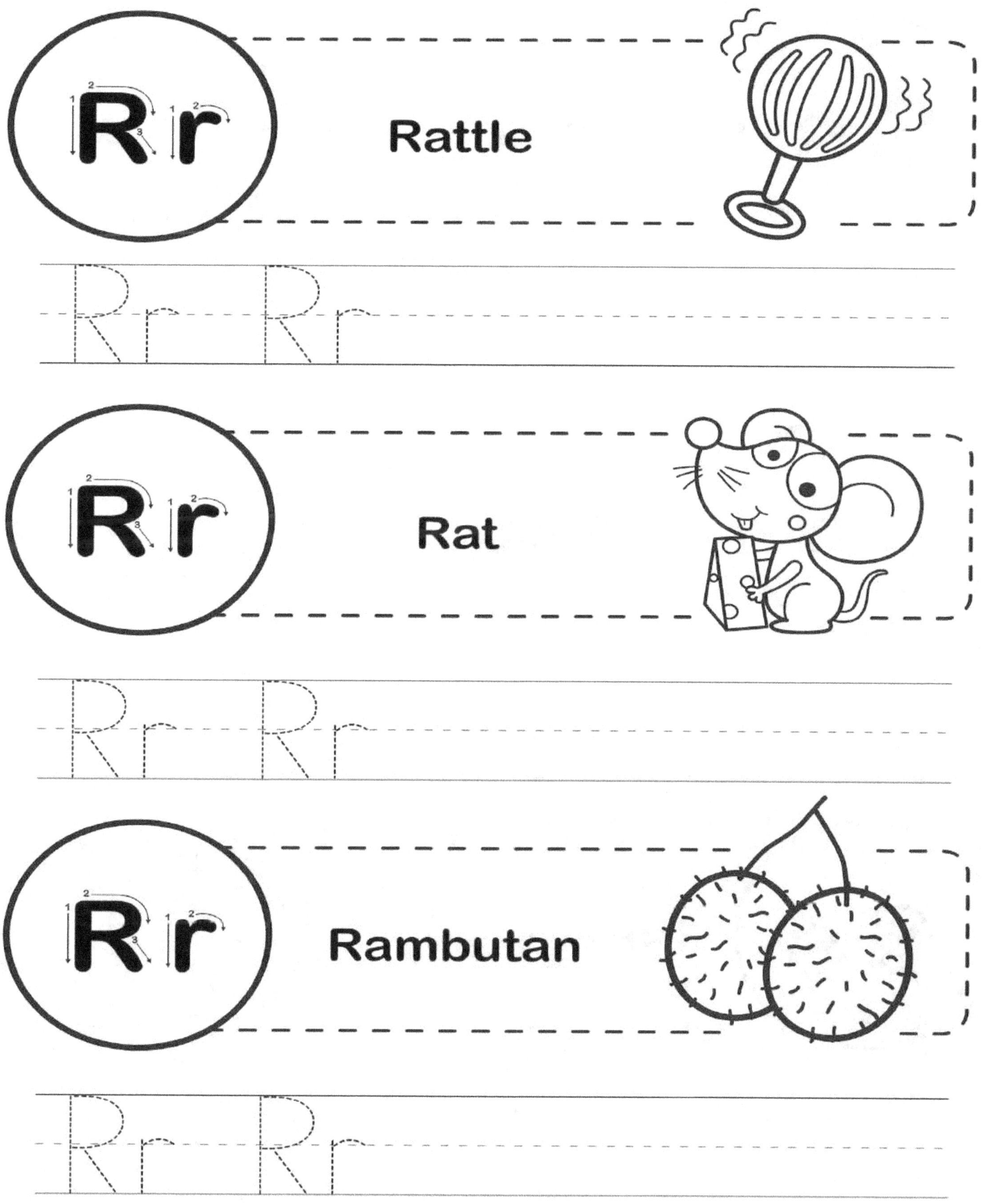

Rr
Rattle
Rr
Rat
Rr
Rambutan

S s
Star
S s
Snake
S s
Strawberry

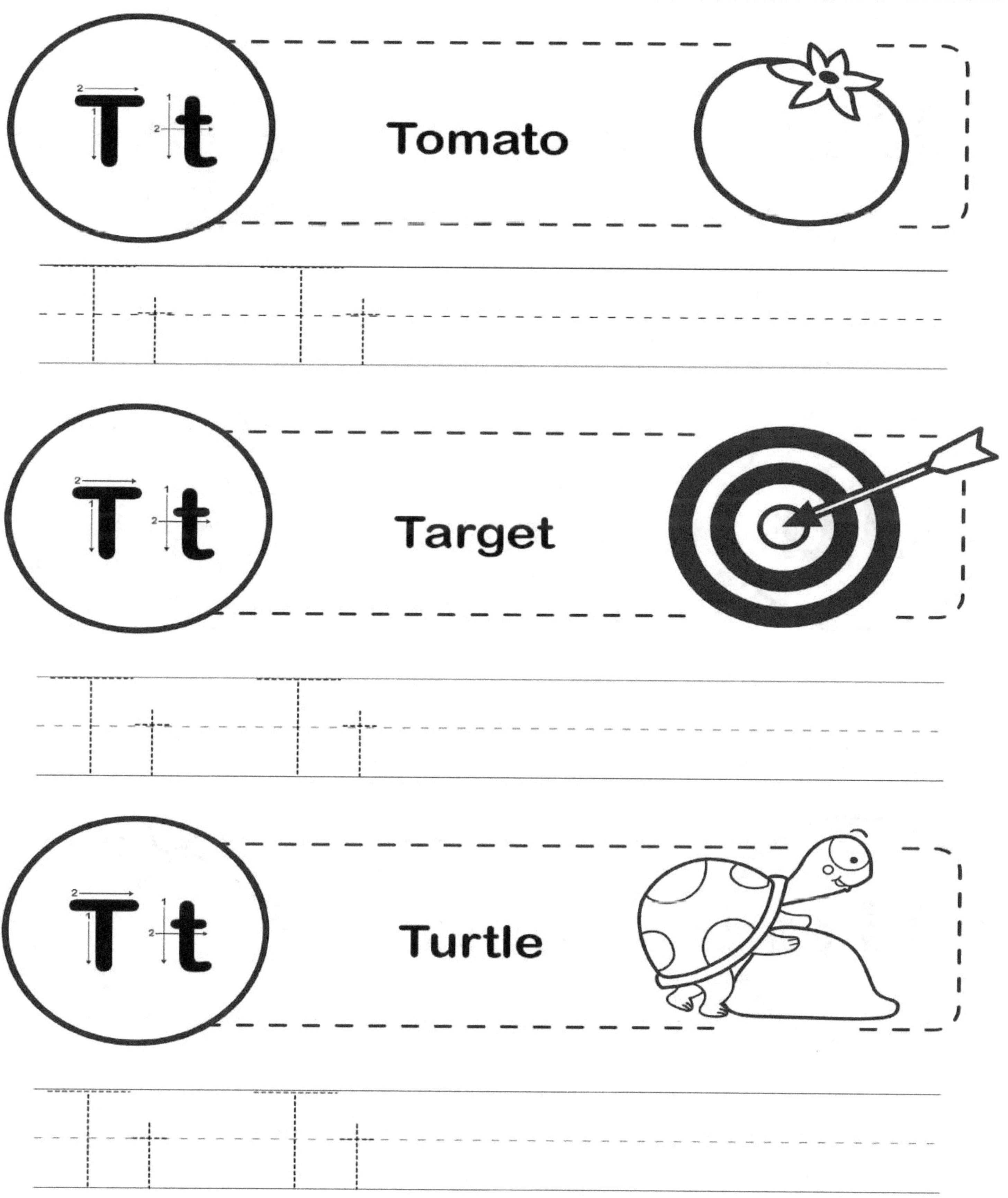

Tomato

Target

Turtle

Read, Trace, Write and read the words again. Color the picture.

U u
Unicycle
U u
Unicorn
U u
Ugli fruit

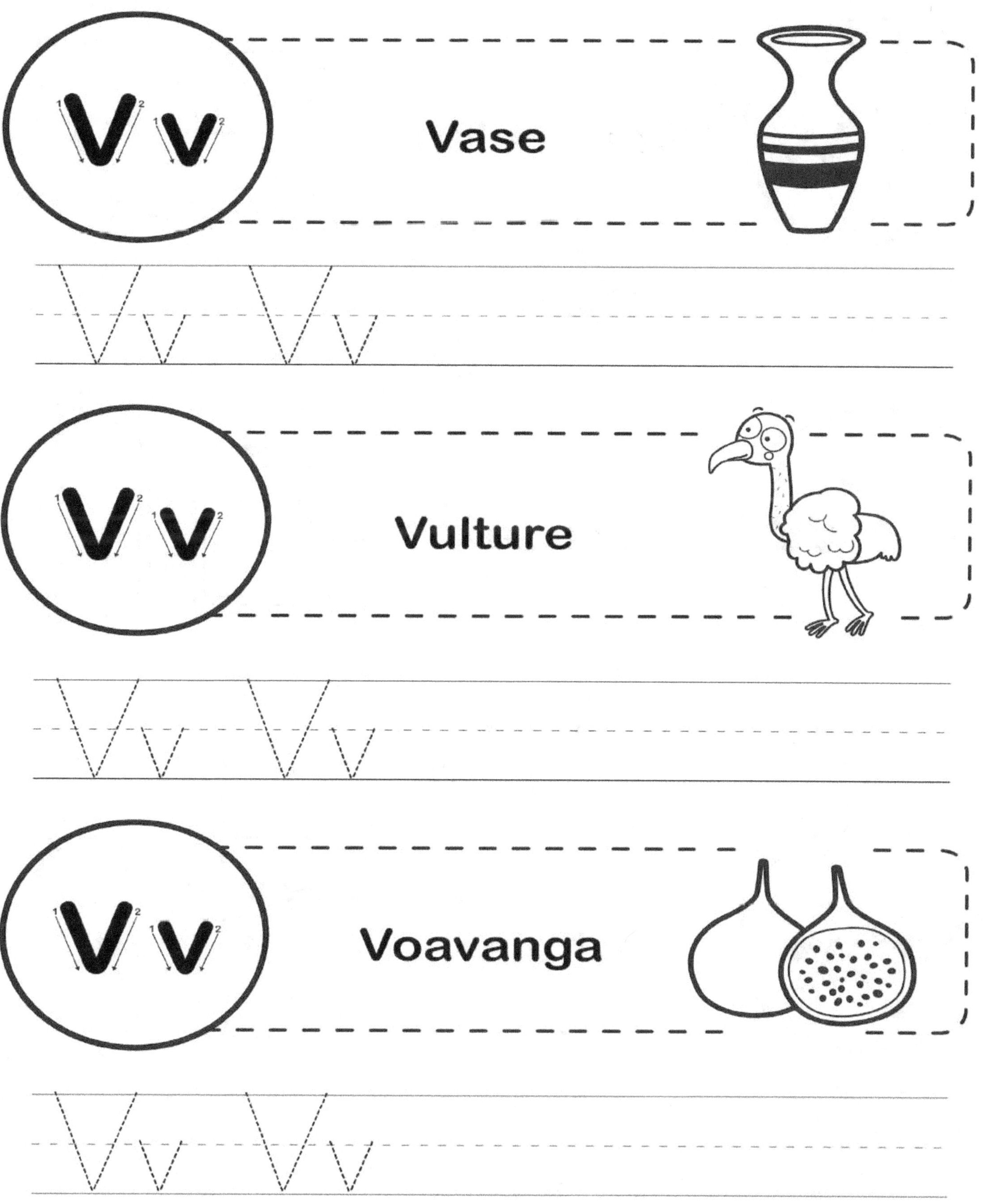

Vase

Vulture

Voavanga

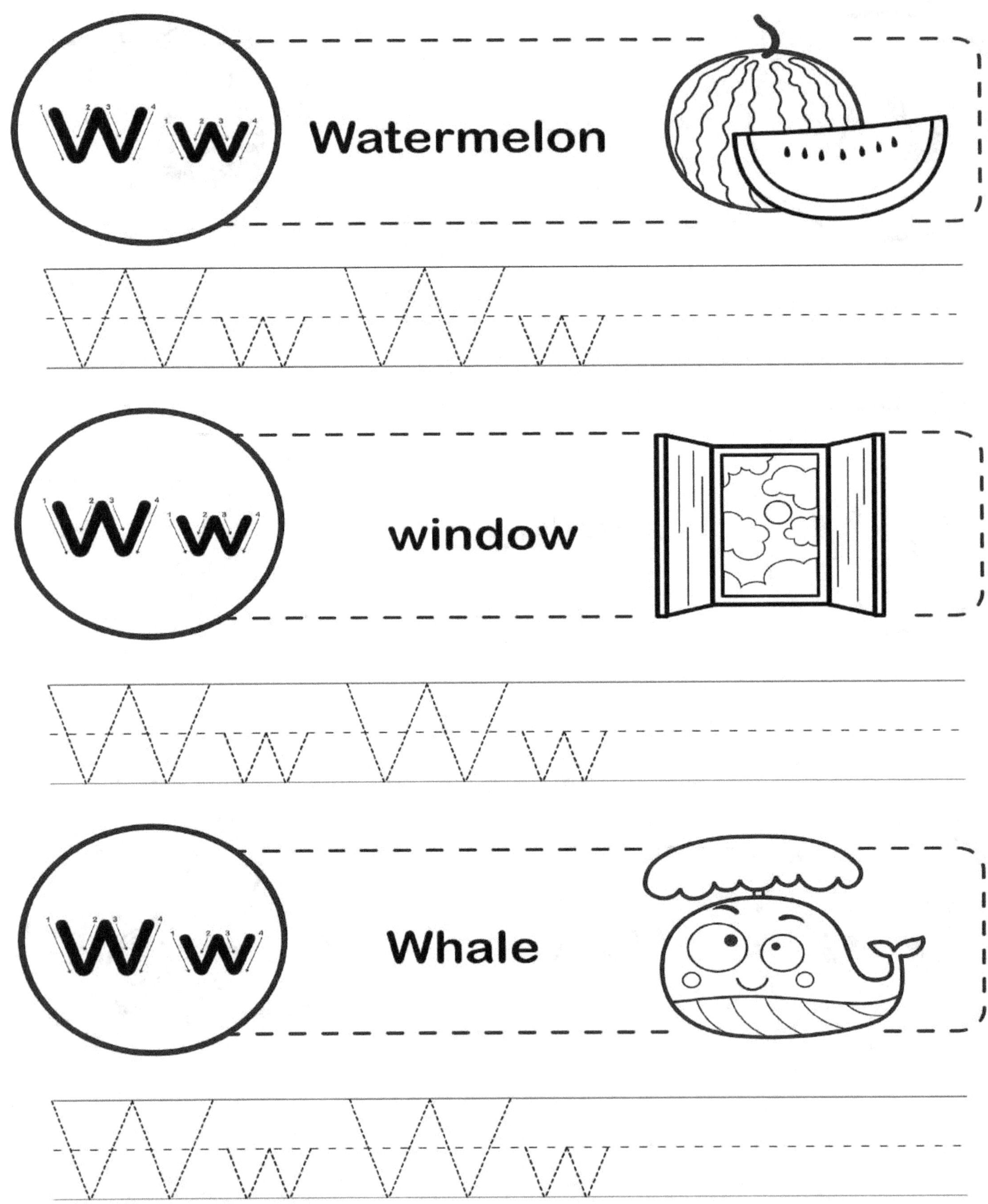
W w
Watermelon
W w
window
W w
Whale

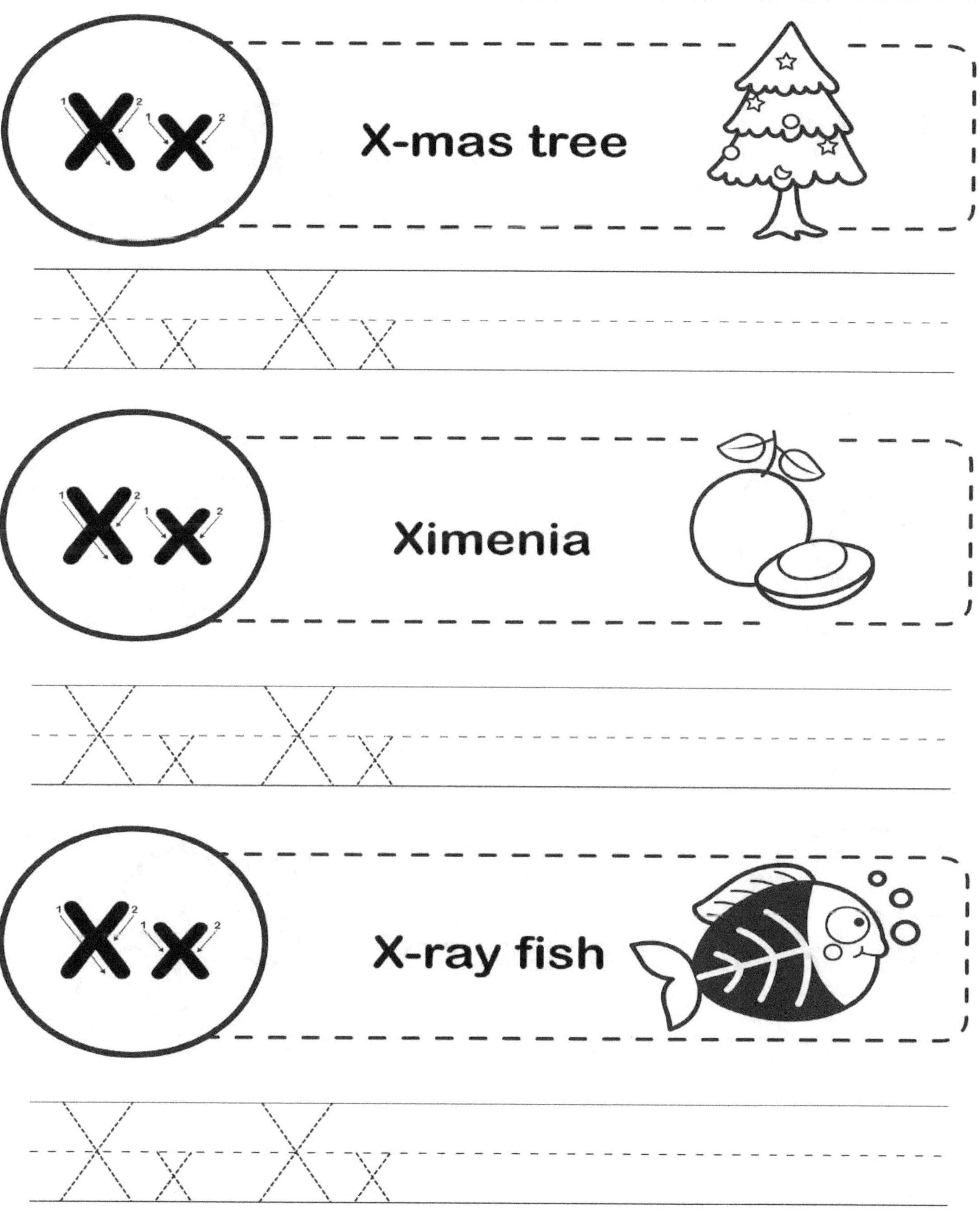
X x
X-mas tree
X x
Ximenia
X x
X-ray fish

Yelk

Yak

Youngberry

Z z

Zoom

Z z

Zebra

Z z

Zapote

Learn to Spell Animals

B
E
E

Learn to Spell Animals

Learn to Spell Animals

Learn to Spell Animals

Learn to Spell Animals

Learn to Spell Animals

A
E
T
P
R
I
C R LL A

Learn to Spell Animals

Learn to Spell Animals

Learn to Spell Animals

N
K
A
O
R
A G O

Learn to Spell Animals

Learn to Spell Animals

Q
I
U
L
A

Learn to Spell Animals

Learn to Spell Animals

C
U
H
N
R   I

Learn to Spell Animals

Learn to Spell Animals
E
T
L
V
U
U
R

Learn to Spell Animals

Learn to Spell Animals

Learn to Spell Animals

Learn to Spell Animals

Learn to Spell Animals

Learn to Spell Animals

Learn to Spell Animals

Learn to Spell Animals

Learn to Spell Animals

Learn to Spell Animals

Learn to Spell Animals

O
D
H
I
L
P
N

Learn to Spell Animals

W L E

H

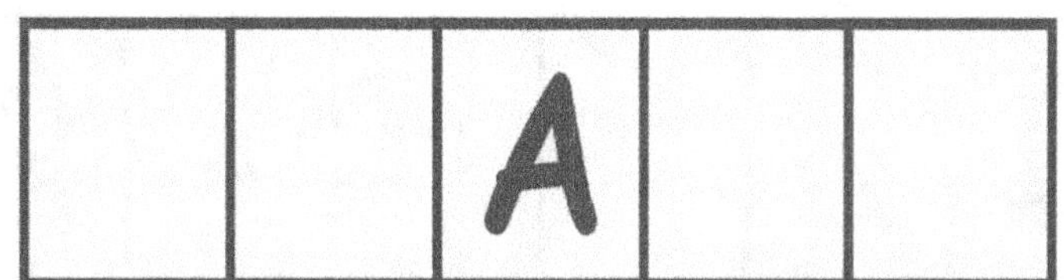

		A		

Learn to Spell Animals

A
G
U
A
J
R

Learn to Spell Animals

Learn to Spell Animals

Learn to Spell Animals

Learn to Spell Animals

Learn to Spell Animals

Learn to Spell Animals

Learn to Spell Animals

M
E
A
L
C

Learn to Spell Animals

Learn to Spell Animals

G
L
A
E
E

Learn to Spell Animals

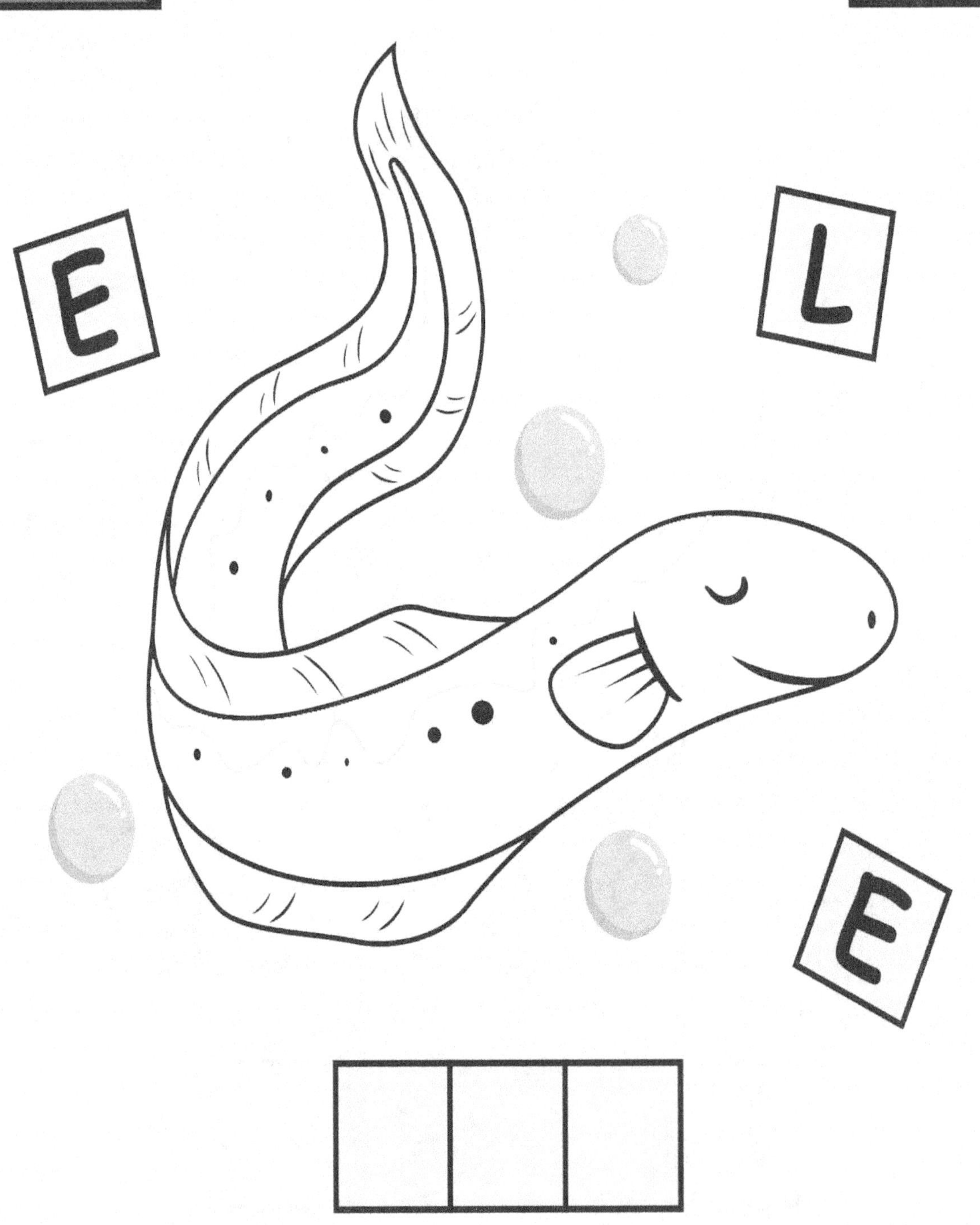

Learn to Spell Animals

Learn to Spell Animals

Learn to Spell Animals

Learn to Spell Animals

Learn to Spell Animals

Learn to Spell Animals

g
f
i
f
a
e
r

Learn to Spell Animals
i
u
q
a
l

Learn to Spell Animals

a
n
e
s
k

Learn to Spell Animals

e
g
h
e
h
g
o
d

a
c
t

Learn to Spell Animals

O
W
1

Learn to Spell Animals
n
r
c
u
i
o
n

Learn to Spell Animals